HOW TO
REPRESENT YOURSELF IN COURT & *WIN*

HOW TO
REPRESENT YOURSELF IN COURT & WIN

SIMPLE STEP-BY-STEP ADVICE

JOHN SALMON

KOGAN PAGE

YOURS TO HAVE AND TO HOLD
BUT NOT TO COPY

First published in 1997

Kogan Page Limited
120 Pentonville Road
London N1 9JN

British Library Cataloguing in Publication Data
A CIP record for this book is available from the British Library.
ISBN 0 7494 2183 5

Typeset by Northern Phototypesetting Co. Ltd, Bolton
Printed in England by Clays Ltd, St Ives plc

Contents

About this book

Our present system is too unequal: there is a lack of equality
between the powerful, wealthy litigant and the under–resourced
litigant

Lord Woolf in his report 'Access To Justice', 1996

Today with cutbacks in legal aid and the ever-spiralling costs for using a lawyer, more and more of us are finding great difficulty in obtaining fair treatment in the courts as a consumer, as an employee or as a householder. Many fear going to court without professional assistance and some of those who have been brave enough to go it alone have been humiliated there because, although they understood what the law is, they did not understand how it is applied in practice. How can there be true justice when a person's inability to pay for legal representation outweighs the basic principle of right and wrong? How can an ordinary person without great financial resources assure his or her rights as a private citizen when dealing with a bank, insurance company or some other large corporation which has access to expensive expert legal advice? The answer is both simple and difficult: simple in that one has the right to represent oneself in court, yet difficult because this is not an easy task. The aim of this book is to render this task easier and thereby redress the imbalance of the scales of justice.

Nobody knows just how many people represent themselves in court proceedings today. The absence of such a statistic is surprising given that there are probably well in excess of 500,000 cases each year in which one or more of the parties involved is not represented by a professional lawyer. This number is set to grow rapidly as company directors, accountants and employees are allowed to represent their company in the courtroom.

Obviously it follows that there are no figures detailing the success rate of those who go it alone through the courts; but current estimates suggest that far, far less than half of them obtain a favourable outcome. The reasons for this are many but one of the most important factors is the failure of the non-professional to understand exactly how to conduct and argue their case. That in itself is hardly surprising given the scarce help there is available for anyone struggling on their own through the courts. A handful of books and a few sources of free or cheap advice do exist but nothing that really tells all that one needs to know. There is almost no information about how to prepare your case and present to the court.

Now at this point I should make it clear that I am a music producer, not a lawyer, nor even the kind of person who would normally pay much attention to legal matters. This book only came about because I simply went shopping one day and, without any choice on my part, found myself involved in a five-year-long court battle against a major bank. Earning too much to qualify for legal aid, yet unable to afford a lawyer, I had to choose between settling a debt which I knew I did not owe or defending myself in court. I had no real option but to proceed the hard way against experienced opposition, learning as I went along. At first I had absolutely no idea how to present my case in court or even how to fill out the necessary forms, but eventually I won through and was awarded compensation for my loss of earnings and the time I had spent in court.

During the proceedings I soon learned that you only have rights to the extent that you are prepared to stand up and fight for them. I was appalled by the lack of information and practical help available to the non-professional court user. It was this above all else that helped me decide to write a book for anyone needing to represent themselves in legal proceedings. With the aid of this book you should have no need to suffer the same difficulties I faced.

The objective of this book is to demystify the legal process with a straightforward step-by-step guide. But this is no ordinary theoretical guide. Written with experience of the gamesmanship of professional lawyers and the inadequacies of the system, it not only describes the court procedures, but also gives tips on how to get practical results. It is about *how* to conduct your case and not *what* your case should be. There is not the space here to cover what the law is in every particular situation but a section has been included on how to obtain expert advice and information on any legal topic.

This book, therefore, is for anyone who has to, or just wants to, handle their own legal affairs. This in itself means very hard work. Lawyers get paid high fees because they provide a particular professional service;

thus you will have to be prepared to work at least as hard as a lawyer yourself in order to succeed. Be sure to read the whole of this book first before taking the plunge, including the sections which may not appear to relate directly to your individual case. Often a principle carries over from one type of legal proceedings into another. Remember that every case is very much a one-off in which anything can happen. As long as you are certain you understand the law relating to your case and fully comprehend the necessary procedures, you should not be taken by surprise. But be warned: it can at times feel lonely being your own advocate.

1

A brief introduction to the English legal system

THE COURTS

English law can broadly be divided into two branches: criminal law, which is concerned primarily with issues of law and order; and civil law which in general relates to private disputes where no crime is alleged. Although there is some overlap between these two branches, criminal and civil legal proceedings take place in different courts with different rules and procedure. Criminal proceedings are almost always commenced in a magistrates' court although the more serious cases are usually transferred to the Crown Court. Civil cases can be further subdivided into divorce and family matters on one hand, with other issues such as the sale of goods, housing, breach of contract and debt on the other. Civil and family business is usually heard in a county court, family court or divorce court with the High Court hearing only certain cases, for example where very large sums of money are involved. Certain everyday civil and family matters can also be dealt with by the magistrates' courts.

Different types of judges preside in these different courts and generally there is a right of appeal to a more senior judge against the decision of any court. Appeals may be heard in the Court of Appeal, although in many instances a preliminary appeal must be made in one of the other courts. Very occasionally an appeal is allowed to the House of Lords but this is normally reserved for issues of special legal or national importance. Figures 1.1 and 1.2 respectively illustrate the hierarchy of the various civil and criminal courts whose functions are described in greater detail in the chapters on court procedure.

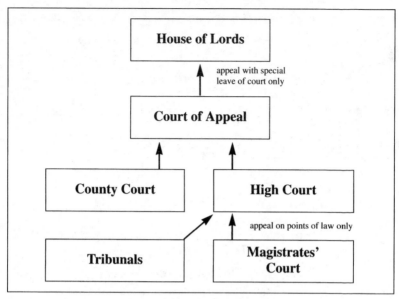

Figure 1.1 *The hierarchy of the civil courts*

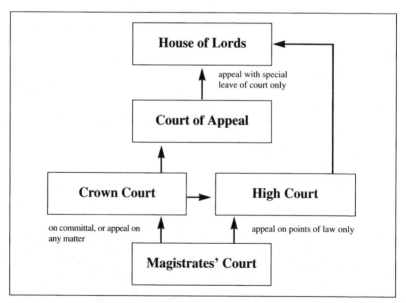

Figure 1.2 *The hierarchy of the criminal courts*

JUDGES AND MAGISTRATES

At the lowest level in the magistrates' courts it is usual to find two or three lay magistrates sitting in judgement. These magistrates normally have no formal qualification in law although they are required to attend special training courses organised by the Lord Chancellor's Department, the government department responsible for the administration of justice. Lay magistrates are always assisted by a justice's clerk, a solicitor of several years' standing, who is there to advise on points of law. There are also some professional or 'stipendiary' magistrates, again normally solicitors of some years' experience, who may hear a case alone.

In the county courts the bulk of the casework is dealt with by district judges, who are usually recruited from the ranks of experienced solicitors. The more important cases in the county courts and those in the Crown Court are heard by recorders or by circuit judges. Generally both recorders, who are part-time judges, and circuit judges are selected from barristers, although recently solicitors have also become eligible. Again several years of experience, typically at least seven for a recorder and at least 15 for a circuit judge, are required as a prerequisite.

Senior judges in the High Court are usually appointed from Queen's Counsel barristers or from among the more junior judges. At the top of the hierarchy are the Lord Justices of the Court of Appeal and the Law Lords who sit in the House of Lords. The selection of judges and magistrates is largely in the hands of the Lord Chancellor, either directly, or in some instances in an advisory capacity to the Queen or Prime Minister who actually makes the appointment.

BARRISTERS AND SOLICITORS

The two principal branches of the legal profession have different functions in court proceedings. Barristers, or counsel as they are commonly known, are specialists in advocacy and their primary role is to conduct a trial on behalf of their client. The most senior barristers are called Queen's Counsel and usually have a more junior barrister to assist them whenever they work. Very often barristers do not become involved in court proceedings until shortly before the trial. A barrister may be engaged through a solicitor and it is usually the solicitor who handles all pre-trial matters. In a complicated or difficult case the barrister may become involved at an earlier stage in an advisory capacity.

Sometimes in the county court a solicitor will conduct a trial himself on behalf of a client and recently solicitors have been given the right to present cases in the High Court. However, solicitors are not limited to just court work; indeed the bulk of work they carry out as a whole is of a non-contentious nature and includes such things as conveyancing, wills and business contracts. Very often much of their preparatory work is actually done by trainee solicitors or legal executives employed and supervised by the solicitor.

Both barristers and solicitors have to undertake two years of training working for their more senior colleagues after first spending usually two years in an academic study of the law, often with a law degree as well. Although these are the only professions strictly dedicated to law they are by no means the only professionals one finds at work in court proceedings. Accountants and other executives will regularly handle their company's legal affairs including actions in the county court. Recent changes in practice relating to small claims in particular mean that nowadays anyone involved in such court proceedings may be accompanied a non-lawyer who can speak on their behalf. A number of trades unions and other similar societies provide excellent legal representation for their members to assist with work-related disputes.

THE LAW AND HOW IT IS APPLIED

English law is very complex, having developed gradually over the centuries. Much of the law is not set down in the form of a comprehensive written code as it is in many other countries but exists as a patchwork of so-called 'common law' and statutes. Unlike statutes which give a written framework to specific areas of the law, common law relies on the principle of precedent. In other words, there is no direct written embodiment of many aspects of the law; instead judges are obliged to follow certain principles laid down in the earlier judgements of the superior courts. This means a judge in a county court or in the High Court is bound to follow the principle behind any judgement, known as the *ratio decidendi*, of any previous similar case decided by a superior court such as the Court of Appeal or the House of Lords. It is customary when quoting any precedent to refer to any published law report which describes the case in question. Very often somewhat conflicting precedents exist and it is up to a judge to decide each case on its individual merits. Almost invariably he will moderate or even adapt a legal precedent to arrive at a decision that he thinks is just, equitable and fair. This measured application of the law is called *jurisprudence* and even when applying statutes which theoretically override common law some degree of such judicial interpretation is the norm.

A good example of how common law works in practice can be found in the way a principle known as 'the remoteness of damage' is applied to cases of breach of contract. This principle which delimits the scope of the damages for which a defendant is liable was expounded in the famous case of *Hadley v Baxendale* [1854] 9 Ex 341 in the statement:

> where two parties have made a contract which one of them has broken, the damages which the other party ought to receive in respect of such breach of contract should be such as may fairly and reasonably be considered as either arising naturally, ie according to the usual course of things, from such breach of contract itself, or such as may reasonably be supposed to have been in the contemplation of both parties, at the time they made the contract as the probable result of a breach of it.

In other words it limited the application of the wider principle that any compensation should, as far as possible, put the innocent party in the same situation they would have been in if the other party had not broken the terms of the agreement between them. Only damages arising in an ordinary manner and in normal circumstances, or those which had been specifically contemplated by both parties at the time of making the contract, were awardable.

For nearly 100 years this was the basis on which judges decided how much damages to award for claims of breach of contract. In 1949 this changed as a result of the judgement in the case of *Victoria Laundry v Newman Industries* [1949] 2 KB 528; [1949] 1 All ER 997, in which it was decided that the criteria for calculating damages beyond those which arise naturally should be based upon what is *reasonably foreseeable* at the time of entering in to the contract. This is only common sense because the old rule put an emphasis on contemplating breaking a contract whereas in reality most parties agreeing a contract would contemplate carrying out the contract rather than breaking it.

More recently the Court of Appeal has decided in the cases of *The Heron* [1969] AC 350 and *H Parsons (Livestock) v Uttley Ingham* [1978] 1 All ER 525 that damages for breach of contract are allowable where the manner in which the damages arise is foreseeable even if the precise amount of the damage itself is not. Thus the law has developed: whereas 100 years ago damages were 'too remote' to be awarded if they were not contemplated at the time of a contract being made, nowadays they are only considered as being 'too remote' if the way in which they arise is not reasonably foreseeable. This does not mean, however, that the old rule in *Hadley v Baxendale* is obsolete. Far from it: damages that are not reasonably foreseeable may still be awarded because special circumstances relating to a contract may have been discussed, and thus contemplated, by both parties when the contract was agreed.

Any present-day judge called upon to decide whether any damages claimed are too remote to be awarded will usually refer back to these cases to help reach his decision. Note, however, that the English legal system puts the judge under no obligation to consider any particular case or legal principle unless it is brought to his attention by one of the parties in the case before him. Thus, if, as often happens, a barrister opposing a litigant-in-person quotes an old case embodying a wide general principle in his client's favour and the litigant-in-person is unable to reply by quoting another case which contradicts, overrules or modifies the principle in the former case, then the barrister's client may well win on that point of law unless the judge himself knows about the more up-to-date case.

Understanding exactly how the common law is applied is often a problem for those representing themselves in court. There can be no substitute for reading the law reports themselves to reach an understanding of this important aspect of our system. The law reports mentioned above will provide a good introduction if read in date order.

The application of statute law by the courts follows similar principles to the application of common law in that the wording of the statute has to be interpreted by the court. Again judges are obliged to follow previous interpretations and principles of interpretation laid down by the superior courts. This can sometimes lead to quite surprising results. For example, the Consumer Credit Act 1974 states that a credit agreement 'is not properly executed unless a document ... including all the prescribed terms and conforming to regulations ... is signed and the document embodies all of the terms of the agreement' (section 61(1)); further, that 'regulations ... may in particular require specified information to be included' (section 60(2)) and that a court shall not order the enforcement of an agreement 'unless a document itself containing all the prescribed terms of the agreement was signed' (section 127(3)). The regulations in question are the Consumer Credit Regulations and provide lists of what information must be included in any valid consumer credit agreement. This may all seem straightforward despite its long-winded wording, but when faced with credit agreements that have mistakes or omissions in the information required by the statute the courts generally follow the precedent of the case of *Lombard Tricity Finance v Paton* [1989] 1 All ER 918 in which it was ruled that a document complies with the Consumer Credit Regulations if the terms simply convey to the average reader the rights of the parties. In the case I was involved in the judge decided that a consumer credit agreement was properly executed even where much of the information required to be included by the regulations was incorrectly entered on the agreement. Surely if the correct figures are not entered then the necessary information is not included in the document?

This example clearly shows that statutes cannot be read in isolation and that one must refer to common law to understand their application. Despite the fact that they are supposed to represent the definitive statement of the law they can effectively be blunted by case law. The awkward legal wording and ungrammatical English with which the statutes are often drafted only makes matters worse. Parliamentary materials such as a minister's speeches introducing a Bill in the House of Commons may be referred to by a court to decide the intent of any ambiguous legislation.

It is important to note that in practice the law is only really applied through the courts by means of a trial and other legal proceedings. These only commence when someone, be it the police, the Crown Prosecution Service, a local authority or a private citizen, refers a matter to a court. The system is adversarial because it always involves one party in direct opposition to another, each fighting to establish their own version of the truth with the judge as a sort of referee in the middle. It is interesting to note that while the concept of the trial has its origins in the historical 'trial by parley' the modern full trial reflects many aspects of the old 'trial by combat' where each side nominates a champion to fight its cause.

2

Being a litigant-in-person

WHY REPRESENT YOURSELF IN COURT?

There may be many different reasons why anyone might decide to represent themselves in court but one reason above all others remains paramount: the expense. It is not cheap to engage a solicitor particularly as that cost may not always be recoverable in court, even if you win. If a case is of any complexity then there will frequently also be the cost of counsel on top of that of the solicitor. Legal aid to cover a solicitor's fees is now no longer as widely available as it used to be and is now largely limited to people with incomes close to or below the state benefit thresholds. Furthermore, the legal aid assessors have a discretion to withhold assistance if they think a case is not worth fighting. In particular, legal aid can be difficult to obtain for civil cases of a purely financial nature and in many instances the legal aid costs and even state benefits such as incapacity benefit and jobseeker's allowance, received in circumstances relating to a case, must be repaid from one's winnings. Other means of free or cheap access to a lawyer such as through a Citizens' Advice Bureau, a legal advice clinic or the solicitor's fixed-fee interview scheme only allow for limited advice and do not include much, if any, provision for representation in court. Thus for many of us there is no real choice except whether to fight it or forget it, and it is rather hard to do the latter if you are owed a significant sum of money or are being sued by someone else.

Fortunately several present-day court procedures have been simplified to make justice more accessible to those without legal representation. The usual rule that the legal costs of the successful party in civil proceedings are paid by the unsuccessful party has been relaxed for certain types of court action including undefended divorce and small claims of less than £3,000. In these instances only the summons fee and sometimes a witness fee, a loss-of-earnings allowance, and out-of-pocket expenses have to be paid by the 'loser'; generally little, if any, solicitor's costs are awarded even if a solicitor has been used.

Of course it may be that for other reasons one does not want to use a solicitor. Sometimes in a particularly complex situation it may be hard for a solicitor to understand the real issues, especially if it is an unfamiliar field of practice to them. Specialist lawyers tend to be very expensive and are often beyond the scope of legal aid. There are also some litigants-in-person who are simply interested in the prospect of being paid by way of winning costs for their endeavour.

Whatever the motive, anyone considering acting for themselves in court should be aware from the outset that there are certain disadvantages inherent in representing oneself. First and foremost there is the lack of detailed knowledge and practical experience of the law and court procedures. This is something that is not easily overcome but much of the deficit can be made up by reading up on the specific field of law that applies to a case. In the majority of instances a lack of expert knowledge is not likely to be a decisive factor; it is only in cases where larger sums of money are involved that it is likely to be crucial. In fact judges hearing small claims and undefended divorces are very understanding of this problem and will not expect a layman to be fully conversant with the law. However, when facing a barrister in court in a matter worth thousands of pounds no special allowance is made for a litigant-in-person and if one cannot argue the points of law on at least equal terms then one will risk failure.

Another important factor to take into account is the amount of time that has to be dedicated to court proceedings. Not only is there the trial to attend but there may be various preliminary hearings to attend as well as all of the preparatory work. Add to this the time spent familiarising oneself with the law and its procedures, plus any time spent obtaining advice, and it all adds up to significant investment of time. It can be very hard work, and emotionally draining too. And lonely.

On the other hand, a successful litigant-in-person may be awarded legal costs as compensation for the time spent working on a case. This is always at the discretion of the judge and depends on the individual circumstances in question. As a general rule, the award of costs is designed to put the successful party in the financial position it would have been in if a resolution of the dispute had been achieved without the matter going to court. There is as well the tremendous feeling of satisfaction that you can get from succeeding with such an intellectual challenge.

There are a number of sources of assistance for anyone with legal problems; you should be able to find most of them in the *Yellow Pages*, *Thomson's* or the telephone directory. In addition to such 'official' advice agencies, it is often useful to discuss such matters with a respected

Ten ways to avoid going to court

Suing someone, or for that matter being sued, is not the happiest way in which to resolve any problem. Depending on the circumstances there may be alternatives. Here are a few.

Take justified action
If you have yet to pay for goods or services which have not been delivered to your satisfaction, then you are quite entitled to refuse to pay for them or only pay what you think they are worth. Where you have paid by credit card, the card company may be able to refund your money if you inform them of the problem. Any faulty goods supplied to you should be returned to the place where they were bought without delay; this will put you in a stronger position to demand your money back.

Talk to someone in a responsible position
Explain why you are dissatisfied and if the person you talk to can't solve the problem then be prepared to go higher. Don't be afraid to approach the managing director or chairman of a company. Often they will be the best placed to settle any dispute.

Negotiate and be willing to compromise
You have nothing to lose; even if nothing is achieved, it is important to try. You should at least find out how the other party justifies their position. Should the matter eventually reach court it is important to be seen to have acted reasonably throughout the dispute.

Go to an outside authority
You may be able to get the local council trading standards department, the Office of Fair Trading or another government department to take up your complaint. In extreme cases where there is a criminal aspect to the situation, such as fraud, the police can become involved.

Use an established complaints procedure
Depending on the precise nature of your problem there might be a trading organisation or trades union complaints procedure available

to you. Sadly these potentially useful means of resolving problems are rarely advertised so you may have to ask around for information on this.

Try the ombudsman, regulator or watchdog
These have the power formally to take up complaints on your behalf and can order compensatory payments to be made. Complaints should be made formally in writing and must be answered by the other party. Using these services does not usually affect your ultimate right to take the matter to court.

Arbitration
Many employment and trade disputes are settled by this method. Make sure that the arbitrator is fully independent because certain contracts specify that only one of the parties has the right to choose this person. Mediation can be another option but never renounce your ultimate right to have the matter settled in court.

Tell others about your problem
No business wants to lose trade as a result of bad publicity. A consumer group or residents' association might have members who could help you, but sadly the old threat of going to the papers rarely works these days. Private disputes are unlikely to be of interest to the newspapers especially if the dispute involves a big-spending advertiser.

Threaten court proceedings
Very, very often a strong letter stating that you will take the matter to court unless it is settled within 14 or 28 days will bring about a speedy solution to any problem. Let the other side of the dispute know that once a summons is delivered then they become liable for legal costs.

Forget it
Where a claim is small, it may simply not be worth pursuing. In terms of the amount of time taken up, the cost of telephone calls and letters, not to mention the stress, it may be better just to let it go.

friend, relative or colleague. In particular they might be able to help you see the other side of the dispute or suggest alternative solutions. An impartial view should never be disregarded out of hand: it may help you to understand how an independent judge might see the situation. Be honest and not biased with anyone whose advice you seek. Don't hide any unfavourable points: remember that the judge is eventually going hear the other side of the tale.

SOLICITORS AND LEGAL AID

Many, but by no means all, firms of solicitors operate schemes whereby free or very cheap legal help is available. Legal aid is the most well known of these and includes the costs of being represented in court as well as the preparatory work. Strict financial qualification criteria are applied and a case has to be seen by the Legal Aid Board as being both essentially winnable and worthwhile. In practice only those close to or below the qualification levels for income support will receive full legal aid. Anyone with a higher level of income or with more than a certain amount of savings will be expected to pay part or all of the bill, the exact amount depending on individual circumstances. Anybody faced with the possibility of impending legal proceedings should contact a solicitor or Citizens Advice Bureau at the earliest possible moment to determine their eligibility. The solicitor or advisor will be able to help with all aspects of filling in the application form. If you qualify, you might as well use it.

The general criteria for the legal aid means test varies depending on whether the case concerned is civil or criminal. Legal aid is available for most categories of proceedings including appeals, although certain types of case, for example undefended divorce, defamation proceedings and private prosecutions, are not covered. The financial criteria for qualification relate to the amounts of *disposable capital* and the *disposable income* of any applicant and contributions are payable towards the cost of legal representation by those with less modest means. Anyone receiving income support or the income-based jobseeker's allowance will normally qualify for free legal assistance.

The calculation of a person's disposable capital takes into account monies held in bank accounts, savings accounts, national savings, stocks and shares. Money that could be borrowed on the security of insurance policies is also included alongside the realisable value of luxury possessions such as boats, caravans, jewellery, antiques, etc. Where the applicant owns or runs a business, account will be taken of any sum of money which might be withdrawn from it without affecting its viability, profitability or commercial credit. Ordinary household and personal items, including a car, and the value of an owner-occupied house (up to £100,000 in value) are disregarded.

The upper limit for qualification on the basis of disposable capital is currently £6750, except in personal injury cases where there is a higher ceiling of £8560. Anyone with disposable capital in excess of these figures does not qualify for legal aid. Where the disposable capital is below £3000, legal aid may be available subject to satisfying the means test for disposable income. Applicants with disposable capital between these upper and lower thresholds will be expected to pay a full contribution to the cost of their legal representation up to the amount of capital they hold in excess of £3000.

Disposable income is calculated by taking a person's total income including any child benefit, net of tax and national insurance, and then deducting rent or mortgage outgoings, employment expenses (such as fares to work, child-minding fees, union dues etc), council tax and maintenance payments. Certain pensions, the disability living allowance and attendance allowance are disregarded in this calculation. A further set amount in respect of the living expenses of the applicant and of each dependant (approximately 150 per cent of the relevant income support allowance) is then deducted and the result, expressed as an annual figure, is compared against upper and lower threshold limits. Subject to satisfying the means test for disposable capital, legal aid is available for those with a disposable income of less than £2563 *per annum*. The upper limit for qualification is £7595 (£8370 for personal injury cases) and between the limits a monthly contribution equivalent to one-thirty-sixth of the excess over the lower limit is payable.

A further contribution to one's legal costs, known as the *statutory charge*, will normally have to be made out of any damages or other monetary settlement that results from the legal action. Certain money awards are exempt from this general rule including maintenance payments and the first £2500 of any divorce or matrimonial settlement.

All civil applications for legal aid are also subject to a *merits test* and assistance will generally be refused where an applicant is seen to have little chance of success or where:

1. the claim is small (eg below the £3000 limit for small claims in the county court);
2. the benefits of the claim might be outweighed by the cost of the action;
3. the case is a defended divorce where a marriage is accepted as having broken down;

4. the case is for repossession where the amount of arrears is not in dispute and an immediate possession order is unlikely to result;

5. the other party has no financial means to satisfy any judgement; or

6. the applicant would get no real benefit from the action.

Legal aid will also be refused where it appears that the applicant has other rights or facilities that would make legal aid unnecessary or there is a reasonable expectancy of receiving financial or other help from a union or other organisation of which the applicant is a member. Where this is the case the applicant will be expected to make use of these other rights, facilities or help.

Sometimes the Legal Aid Board, who are charged with determining an applicant's entitlement, will issue a *limited certificate* which will allow legal aid up to a certain stage of preparation. This allows a solicitor, for example, to interview witnesses and review any other evidence before making a decision on the merits of a case. If after consulting a barrister the case appears winnable then legal aid will probably be extended to include court proceedings. Don't necessarily be put off taking court action if a lawyer pronounces your case as 'not winnable' because it is very hard for a solicitor to get a full understanding of a complex dispute from the basis of a short interview. I found myself in exactly this situation and eventually won in court; so might you. If you know you have a strong case then you can still take it to court yourself as a litigant-in-person.

It is worth mentioning here that many of the legally aided civil litigants who are required to make contributions towards the cost of their legal representation withdraw from the court proceedings before any judgement is reached. This is unfortunate because all of these cases will have been judged to have a reasonable chance of success under the merits test. If you are receiving legal aid but cannot afford the contributions you have every right to take over the running of the case yourself at no further cost. All you need to do is fill out a simple form for the court office and ask the solicitor for all of the relevant paperwork. From then on the procedure is exactly the same as for any other litigant-in-person as described in the following chapters of this book.

Criminal legal aid, while not subject to a merits test, is subject to means testing and contributions along similar lines to civil legal aid. There is no upper threshold for disposable income or disposable capital; otherwise the criteria are pretty much the same. Legal aid should be applied for well ahead of any hearing but can also be applied for at any bail hearing, committal hearing or trial simply by asking the clerk of the court. Upon receipt of the completed application form the magistrate, clerk or judge has the power to order immediate assistance in the form of advice and representation by a *duty solicitor* and there is no means test or contribution for this. However, any further work, in or out of court, that is necessary will be means-tested and subject to contributions. In Crown Court cases an initial refusal to grant legal aid can effectively be appealed against by means of a further application made to the judge at the time of trial.

In addition to full legal aid, the Legal Aid Board operates two other useful schemes known as *Assistance By Way Of Representation* and the *Green Form Scheme*. The former of these, commonly called by its acronym, *ABWOR*, has the same means test criteria for disposable capital to civil legal aid but has a higher disposable income ceiling of around £147 per week. It is automatically available to those who qualify for *Green Form* assistance although applicants with a disposable income of over £61 per week must pay a one-third contribution. *ABWOR* may cover immediate urgent family proceedings in the magistrates' court or the High Court as well as employment (industrial tribunal) and social security appeals. County court cases are not usually covered and standard legal aid should be sought for such proceedings. A magistrates' court or county court may of its own motion authorize *ABWOR* where a litigant is not receiving nor has been refused legal aid and the representation is by a solicitor who is already within the precincts of the court for another matter. Additionally the court must be satisfied that the hearing should proceed that day and that the person would not otherwise be suitably represented.

The *Green Form Scheme* which is granted on a basis similar to legal aid is available to those on low incomes. The qualification criteria are stricter than those for legal aid, with disposable capital of £1000 and disposable income of £61 per week being the cut-off points. Persons in receipt of income support automatically qualify provided they are within the disposable capital criterion. Again there is the statutory charge whereby the legal costs are deducted from any settlement reached with the assistance of the Green Form Scheme. This recovery cannot be made where the solicitor is no longer giving advice or assistance at the time of the settlement. As well as allowing for general advice and assistance from a lawyer the scheme includes representation in court for certain categories of proceedings, most notably actions relating to maintenance payments and domestic violence, sometimes on the basis of a *McKenzie friend* (see p 51) in cases where there is no standard legal aid available. Other principal areas covered are:

1. personal injury cases including the taking of initial instructions by a solicitor and early preparatory work, including a full legal aid application;

2. criminal cases:
- initial help inside a police station by a *duty solicitor*; this is neither means-tested nor contributory;
- subsequent work outside the police station; and
- private prosecution for assault or harassment where standard legal aid is not available
3. planning and property matters including general advice, letter writing and negotiating;
4. welfare benefits cases; and
5. immigration cases.

More universally available is the fixed-fee 'low-cost' interview where a half-hour consultation can be arranged for a smallish sum, at present usually around £25. Beyond this first session normal solicitor's fees are charged. Almost any legal matter can be covered by this scheme.

Recent changes in the law now allow for a lawyer to take on personal injury cases and waive the costs to the client in return for a share of the winnings. As yet this type of arrangement is rare among solicitors and such 'no-win no-fee' services, described on p 17, are generally offered by non-lawyers.

CITIZENS ADVICE BUREAUX

Open to everyone, with branches throughout the country, these bureaux generally provide an excellent service across a wide range of affairs. They hold information on almost every type of problem that can beset a private citizen. The standard of legal advice and help varies from branch to branch. Perhaps the worst criticism that can be levelled at them is that they are overstretched and underfunded and thus have to rely somewhat on staff with little experience of the courtroom. However, access to consult a solicitor free of charge can usually be arranged but normally by appointment only. Get in touch with them at the first opportunity as you may have to wait a few weeks for your consultation. Representation by a barrister can sometimes also be arranged where a case warrants it.

LOCAL LAW CENTRES

Local law centres are funded by local authorities and tend to cover only particular areas of the law. Ask at your local town hall, civic centre or public library for details. The staff generally include qualified solicitors and barristers who can deal with contentious and non-contentious matters, although in-court representation is not always covered. They can sometimes be especially good at solving problems to do with housing, immigration or consumer issues. Other legal advice centres are run by volunteer solicitors where the advice given is usually limited to non-court work. However, they can be useful for appraising any problem prior to the start of court proceedings.

NO-WIN NO-FEE SERVICES

Very recently a number of services have started up in several cities advertising 'no-win no-fee' assistance for legal matters including employment problems. The cost of the work they undertake for their clients comes solely from what they manage to obtain as a settlement on their client's behalf, charged either as a fixed fee or as a percentage of the settlement itself. The rules of court make little provision for the award of legal costs for work done by a non-lawyer and this means that the cost of such a service cannot be recovered in the same way as a solicitor's costs. However, many of these companies do provide a very competent service even if, at the end of the day, you do end up with less money than if you took the matter to court or tribunal yourself. If you are too busy, or too daunted, to entertain the prospect of acting for yourself, these services can represent a valid option. They are on the whole much cheaper than hiring a solicitor although eligibility for legal aid and the possibility of winning legal costs can redress this imbalance. Remember that should you lose a case you may still be liable for the legal costs of the other side.

OTHER SOURCES OF HELP

Trades unions, action groups, social services and even the police can be useful sources of information depending on the circumstances. Some organisations such as trades unions and action groups will even provide legal representation for disputes within their field of activity. Some trading organisations offer mediation services for the resolution of consumer problems. Other bodies such as the AA, the RAC and insurance companies can also provide help. Some insurance policies include a provision for professional legal expenses in certain categories of civil disputes. Go direct to the insurer, union representative or other responsible person. A number of organisations who are potential sources of help are included in Appendix 4. Don't be afraid to ask.

Court staff are able and usually quite willing to help anyone involved in court proceedings with procedural matters. They also can supply a number of well-written free leaflets explaining certain aspects of being a litigant-in-person. Obviously the staff have to remain impartial and therefore cannot give specific detailed personal advice but in reality they do provide invaluable help for many non-professional court users. However, it should be remembered that while the court staff should always be able to prescribe which forms may be filed in any certain situation they are not officially authorised to give anything other than general assistance.

As well as being an indispensable source of information in the form of books, many libraries have lists of local solicitors and other legal services. Some have Citizens Advice Bureaux self-help files too. Access to a well-stocked library is a must for any serious litigant-in-person and before matters even get to court you should make enquiries with your local branch library who should be able to point you in the right direction. While not every local library has a good law section, specialised law books can always be obtained on inter-library loan for a small reservation fee. Note that while your local library will be able to provide specialised texts from other sources on inter-library loan, this facility is often very slow and short-term and there is no guarantee that books will be provided for you promptly enough to be of any use. Some reference libraries in the larger cities have excellent law collections and even stock copies of the major law reports. Other possibilities include university libraries and private collections such as the Law Society library and the Law Lending library in London which can be used for a fee.

3

Civil procedure in the County Court

BEFORE THE START OF PROCEEDINGS

No one should ever let a situation reach court without first seriously trying to negotiate a settlement of the dispute. Going to court should always be seen as the last resort when all other options have been exhausted.

- Approach the other party with a tone of compromise.
- Try to discover how they justify their position.
- Try explaining yours.
- When dealing with more than one person insist on talking to the most senior.
- Don't get angry or personal.
- Accept mediation as long as it does not affect your ultimate right to go to court.

Even if you cannot reach a compromise, any information you can obtain at this stage will be invaluable later when preparing arguments for trial. Be sure to keep all correspondence and other documents relating to the problem; they may prove useful later on. Read up on the specific field of law or take expert advice. Could you or they convince a judge to see one side or the other of the argument?

- Consider what evidence there is to set before the court.
- Are there any telling documents, or photographs or witnesses?
- How can you prove that you are right and the other side wrong?
- If you do not have enough evidence then see if more can be found.
- Could it be argued that you have failed to minimise your loss?
- Start thinking about how to summarize your position in writing. It is

one thing to know that you are in the right, it is something else entirely to convince a judge of that fact.

If you are considering taking someone else to court be sure that they are the right person or party. If you sue the wrong party you will lose your summons fee and probably have to pay costs to them. Be especially careful when dealing with companies and partnerships; business structures can be very complex and the legal name of the business may be very different from the trading name. You will need to have the registered office address of a company or the names of the partners constituting a partnership. Any registered office address can be obtained from Companies House (see Appendix 3) of from the publication, *Companies Registration Directory*, which some libraries keep. If the precise identity of the business is not clear from any relevant paperwork (which it should be by law) then deliver a written request to the business premises asking for this information. If this fails, then contact the local trading standards office or the Citizens Advice Bureau, for the company has committed a further offence by not responding to your request. Don't be naive about this sort of thing: if someone has been carrying on business unscrupulously then they are not going to make it easy for anyone to take them to court. From the outset be aware that some people will just up and vanish or liquidate their business once they know a serious court action is pending.

Another consideration to be taken into account before the commencement of proceedings is the ability of the other party to pay you any money that might be awarded by the court. If they are bankrupt or in liquidation or close to it you may win your case but not receive any compensation for the time and money spent fighting it.

Once you have made up your mind to proceed to court do so quickly. There are strict time limits within which proceedings must be started which vary according to the type of case.

TIME LIMITS

Most civil claims in the county court and the High Court must be brought within six years of the event giving rise to the claim: for example, six years from the date on which a debt became due and unpaid, a contract broken, or the date when unsatisfactory goods or services were provided. This limit, for all money claims, contract and tort cases, also covers most civil matters in the magistrates' court (such as council tax arrears and certain trading standards cases), and is subject to exceptions where action during the limits has not been possible. For example, where there has been damage which could not have been evident at the time of the original contract, an action might be brought up to three years after the discovery of the damage. An overall limit of 15 years is applicable in such 'latent' damage cases even where there has been deliberate concealment of the damage by the defendant. Special leave of court must always be applied for to commence proceedings outside the standard six-year limit. The same provision also applies where a time extension is sought on the grounds that the death, disability or illness of a party has precluded the possibility of legal action within that limit.

Shorter time limits are applied in personal injury cases where the time limit for commencing an action is three years. (Note that there is a special pre-proceedings protocol for such cases which is explained in Appendix 2.) Matters of civil liability, such as obligations due under orders of court or statutes are subject to a two-year limit. If there is any doubt about the date from which the period is calculated, it is defined as the date on which the plaintiff first had cause to take legal action. The limitation periods not only affect one's right to commence proceedings but can also limit the right to amend pleadings during the later stages of procedure where an amendment is sought after the expiry of the relevant period, particularly if the amendment seeks to establish a new aspect to a claim. In cases involving a counterclaim or third-party notice the limitation period is calculated back from the date of the initial claim which brought the matter into court.

DEALING WITH THE COURT OFFICE

Occasionally you may experience some delays or other administrative difficulties with your case. While it is usually all right to let matters take their course, there may be times when you wish to chase things up at the court office. If you need to do so then the following guidelines may prove helpful:

1. Whatever you have to say to the court office put it in writing. Always quote the case number and the names of the parties. If you wish to communicate on two different unrelated points then write two separate letters otherwise you might find that some of the points you raise are ignored. Remember that the court office can only deal with procedural matters and cannot directly interfere with the decision of a judge which can only be varied by that judge or another on appeal or application.

2. If you can take the letter to the court office in person then do so. If not then post it; telephoning is often a waste of time. Make sure the letter is clearly dated and if you do go in person get the name of the person you give it to. Always keep a copy yourself.

Ten things to remember about small claims in the county court

The small claims procedure in the county court is a simplified form of legal action for resolving disputes that are of monetary value of less than £3000 (disputes involving greater sums of money can be dealt with if both sides agree).

How to make a claim
All you need to do is to visit your local county court and ask for a summons form. This simple form must be completed with details of the parties concerned, brief reasons for the claim and must also specify the amount of money claimed. A fee of between £10 and £80 is payable to the Court (cheques should be made out to Her Majesty's Paymaster General) and depends on the exact amount of monetary compensation, known as *damages*, in question.

The defendant's response
The person or company against whom you have made your claim, called the *defendant*, will be sent a copy of your claim and has 14 days in which to respond to the court by admitting and offering to settle the claim, or by denying all or part of it. Where your claim is denied they must file a defence which states why they dispute it. The defendant may also make a claim against you called a counterclaim. The court will send you a copy of the defendant's response. If no response is received within the 14 days you can ask the court to enter *summary judgement* in your favour. However, this can be set aside if for some reason the defendant did not receive the summons.

What happens next?
After receiving a defence to the claim, the case will be transferred to the court in the district where the defendant lives or does business. You will be sent a letter from the court giving directions for pre-trial procedures such as the disclosure of evidence. This will require you to send copies, to the other party, of any documents or other evidence you wish to rely on at the hearing. You should also send them a summary of any witnesses or experts whose testimony you wish to

present. The court will then arrange a date for hearing the case and let you know in due course.

The hearing
You must attend the hearing on the date given. If you cannot make it you must let the court know in advance. The hearing is less formal than an ordinary trial.

Help in court
You may have someone with you at the court to support and help you. This can be a friend, a relative or perhaps a union representative. They may only speak for you with the permission of the judge.

Witnesses and experts
You can call witnesses and an expert to support your case. Instead of attending court their evidence can be presented as a signed witness statement or as a sworn *affidavit*.

The judge is independent
Small claims are normally heard by a district judge who should be addressed 'Your Honour'. Be polite, even if you strongly disagree with things said at the hearing. Try not to interrupt or get angry. You will have the chance to put your side of the argument.

The judgement
The judge's decision is based on the evidence presented before him. He only knows what he is told at the hearing. It is up to you to bring enough evidence and explain your side of the dispute fully.

Legal costs
The award of legal costs is limited to a maximum of £50 for each witness (£200 for an expert) plus the summons fee.

Enforcement
The judge's decision can be enforced in the same way as any other court order, with a bailiff's warrant or with deductions from the defendant's bank account or pay.

3. If you receive no reply within a reasonable period, say seven to ten days, then chase the matter up. Go back to the court, or telephone and ask to talk to the same person as you spoke to before. Be prepared to leave an additional copy with the court in case they have lost the original or can't find it.
4. If after a few more days you have still had no reply then you should not hesitate to contact the supervisor or even the Chief Clerk of the court office. Under the Courts Charter section of the Citizen's Charter you have the right to a reply *within* 14 days.
5. Where no response is received within the 14 days then an official complaint in writing should be made to the Chief Clerk of the court. If this brings no immediate result then go higher to the Lord Chancellor's Department at Trevelyan House, 30 Great Peter St, London SW1P 2BY. This is the government department which deals with the administration of the courts and has the power to award compensation for mistakes at the court office which leave you out of pocket.

It is worth bearing in mind that many of the day-to-day procedural matters of the court are dealt with by junior district judges. Therefore if you are unhappy with the outcome of any procedural decision you may well have the right of appeal to a more senior judge (see Chapter 7, pp 129–30).

COURT RULES AND REGULATIONS

In theory all court actions are subject to strict rules of procedure. The rules governing county court proceedings can be found in their entirety in the *County Court Practice* which also has explanatory notes illustrating their application. Additionally the book includes extracts of the Rules of the Supreme Court, that is the rules of High Court procedure, as well as extracts of a number of important statutes. It is a provision of the County Court Rules that wherever those Rules have no specific provision for any circumstances arising in a county court, the Rules of the Supreme Court should generally be adopted. It is worth noting that certain statutes require specific procedures to be followed in court and sometimes even before the commencement of court proceedings. A comprehensive outline of these special procedures can be found in the various volumes of *Atkin's Court Forms* and Butterworth's *Encyclopedia of Forms and Precedents* both available at good law libraries.

COMMENCEMENT OF PROCEEDINGS: THE SUMMONS

The first step is always to go to the local county court and explain very briefly what claim you want to make. The county court has a jurisdiction that covers practically all civil matters including breach of contract, bankruptcy, debt, landlord and tenant actions, personal injury cases and repossession proceedings. Money claims, however, are, at present, limited to a maximum value of £50,000 and claims for any larger amount must be made in the High Court.

The court staff will be able to supply you with the correct forms for your claim and indicate what fee must accompany the completed forms. This fee depends on the amount of money claimed, known as *damages*, or the type of other remedy sought if there is no money claimed. The courts also have a number of explanatory leaflets which must be in great demand because they often seem to have run out. The court fees can sometimes be waived for those on very low incomes.

Note that while you may start an action in a county court of your choice, the case will automatically be transferred to the local county court of the district where the defendant lives, or carries on business, once a defence has been received.

In most cases the proceedings will be commenced by applying for a summons. The application form, Form N1 or Form N201, is quite simple and self-explanatory, requiring the names and addresses of the parties in dispute, the amount of damages claimed and brief details, known as the *particulars of claim*, of the circumstances giving rise to the claim. These particulars should set out the essential elements of the entire case against the defendant and must include all the relevant facts on which you intend to rely to prove your side of the argument. It is recommended that the particulars are typed, or at least written very neatly, on a separate sheet as the relevant space on the summons application is very small and unlikely to be sufficient. Appendix 1, pp 137–55, gives examples of particulars of claim.

If the claim relates to any kind of business activity on your part it is best to start the summons with a very short description of the business and how long the business has been going on. To avoid any confusion between the parties involved in a dispute it is customary to use the term *plaintiff* to describe the party making the claim and *defendant* for the party against whom the claim is made. The paragraphs should be numbered to allow for easy reference during the trial. Thus the first paragraph of a claim might read:

1. The Plaintiff is self-employed and runs a successful grocery business which has been established for over 15 years.

Do not exaggerate or lie, because if the defendant disputes any statement you will have to prove its truth to the judge. The subsequent paragraphs of the particulars of claim should go on to describe in brief detail and in date order the events that took place. If appropriate include a description of the status of the defendant. The particulars of claim should outline only the relevant facts but not go into detailed evidence, which should be saved for the trial. For example the gist of a certain conversation that took place should be included without recounting the whole dialogue. Key facts, such as the existence of a written contract or agreement, any exchanges of letters, any special requirement made known, or other information given to the defendant at the time in question must be recorded. Keep the particulars of claim as simple as possible so that they can be easily and quickly understood by anyone who has to read them. For example, the particulars of claim might continue:

2. On 15 October 1996 the Plaintiff visited the premises of the Defendant, a supplier of refrigeration equipment.
3. On the recommendation of the Defendant, the Plaintiff ordered two cold display cabinets which were delivered on 19 October 1996.
4. In June 1997 food stored in the cold display cabinets went off and had to be thrown away.
5. The Plaintiff notified the Defendant as soon as he was aware of the problem.
6. On 1 July 1997 the Plaintiff asked the Defendant to send an engineer to repair the cabinets but no engineer came and food stored in them continued to spoil.
7. On 31 July 1997 the Plaintiff asked the Defendant to replace the cabinets or reimburse the price paid.
8. The Defendant repeatedly failed to reply to the Plaintiff's requests to discuss the problem.

The final paragraphs of the particulars of claim should include a short statement of the legal principle underlying the claim, details of the damages, a claim for interest, and a claim for the legal costs of the court action:

9. The Plaintiff claims damages on the grounds that the goods supplied by the Defendant were not of satisfactory quality and were unfit for the purpose for which they were sold.
10. The Plaintiff claims damages of £1,700 in respect of the stock that was lost and £1,250 in respect of monies paid to the Defendant for the defective goods.
11. The Plaintiff also claims interest under section 69 of the County Courts Act 1984 at the rate of 8 per cent per annum

from 31 July 1997 to 12 August 1997 being £7.75 and at the daily rate of £0.64 per day up to the date of judgement.
12. The Plaintiff claims the Costs of this Action.

The clause claiming interest looks rather technical but needs to be included in this form if you want to claim interest. If the amount you are claiming is substantial and there has been a substantial delay in the case coming to trial then interest is certainly worth claiming. The usual clause for claiming interest is as follows:

The Plaintiff also claims interest under section 69 of the County Courts Act 1984 at the rate of [8] per cent per annum from [*date of the defendant's default*] to [*date of issue of summons*] being £[*precise amount*] and at the daily rate of £[*amount of interest accruing each day*] per day up to the date of judgement.

The rate of interest is set by the Lord Chancellor's Department and is changed from time to time. The court office will always be able to tell you what the current rate is.

While the statement of a legal principle is bound to be of some difficulty to the inexperienced litigant-in-person, it is important to remember that when it comes to the trial it is the legal arguments and not moral considerations which will be decisive. Besides it would be folly to take a case to court without finding out what the legal rights and wrongs of the situation really are. There are a number of general law books which are good for this kind of information (see Appendix 4, pp 167–69) and expert advice can always be sought.

It is usually best to try a number of test drafts prior to finalising the particulars of claim. Only when you are totally happy with the particulars of claim, and have had someone else read them through to check for mistakes and ease of understanding, should you consider filing them with the court. If the particulars are written on another sheet then it is advisable to put a header on the sheet in case it becomes separated from the application for the summons (see Figure 3.3, p 37).

The completed application for the summons, the particulars of claim and the necessary fee should be taken or sent to your local county court. Payment by cheque should be made out to Her Majesty's Paymaster General or simply HMPG. Cash and postal orders can also be accepted. Don't forget to keep a copy of the summons and the particulars for yourself.

When the court receives the paperwork and the fee it will put the claim on record and assign a case number to it. The court will send a copy of the summons and the particulars of claim to the defendant together with a form listing the alternative ways of responding to it. Once you decide to begin a court action you should keep a diary recording all the work you do on the case. This record will prove invaluable when you make a claim for costs upon winning the case. The matter becomes *sub judice* once the court proceedings have begun and neither you or the other party should *publicly* say, write or otherwise do anything that might prejudice the ability of the court to ensure a fair trial of the case.

WHAT TO CLAIM

The amount of damages claimed should be equivalent to the real loss which has occurred, for example the full amount of a refund for unsatisfactory goods returned to a shop or the full value of an unpaid debt. In cases involving business contracts the damages may include a sum for the loss of profit arising directly as a result of a contract being broken. In personal injury cases the damages may include amounts in respect of any loss of earnings due to the injury, any medical fees that resulted and a sum for the injury itself. Remember that if you are able to reduce or mitigate the loss you have incurred it is important to take this into account (see pp 67–8). Administrative costs, such as those of letters and telephone calls incurred trying to sort out a problem are not generally allowable. A claim for interest prior to the date of commencing court proceedings is not allowable unless there is a formal agreement between the parties that such interest may be claimed (the small print of business contracts often permits this).

It is possible to make a claim without being able to specify the extent of the damages where it is not possible to calculate them accurately at the time of commencing proceedings; such damages are known as *unliquidated damages*. Where a claim relates to the loss of specific profits, perhaps arising from a lucrative contract that cannot be fulfilled, this should be detailed in the statement of claim as an item of *special damage*.

- Identify defendant and defendant's status (individual, company, partnership, etc)
- Explore other means of settlement
- Check legal basis of claim
- Within time limits?
- Is loss mitigated?
- Complete summons form
- Write up particulars of claim (three copies)
- Write up details of losses/damages (three copies)
- Check court fee (£10 to £80 in the small claims court depending on the amount claimed)

Figure 3.1 *Summons checklist*

THE DEFENDANT'S RESPONSE

After receiving a summons and the particulars of claim the defendant normally has 14 days to reply to the court. If no reply has been received by the court after the expiry of this period the plaintiff may ask for *summary judgement* to be entered. If judgement is entered in this way the damages claimed plus the legal costs of the summons become immediately payable. Steps can then be taken to enforce the judgement.

The defendant can, however, make an *application* for the judgement to be *set aside* on the ground for example of being out of the country at the time. Unfortunately some defendants pretend they have not received a summons; therefore it might be advisable for any plaintiff to serve a duplicate copy by recorded delivery post or even deliver it by hand. Where a court summons is served by hand the person delivering should go immediately to the court office and swear an *affidavit of service* which is a sworn statement giving evidence of the delivery. Most court offices have special forms available for this.

A defendant can make one of a number of responses to a summons. Firstly, without making any admission of liability, the defendant can simply pay the amount claimed on the summons and that will be the end of the matter. Alternatively the defendant can admit that he is liable to pay, but dispute the actual amount he has to pay. If part of the amount claimed is not disputed then that amount should be paid immediately, either direct to the plaintiff or in certain circumstances it should be 'paid into court' (see p 39). If all or part of the claim is disputed then the defendant should file a defence with full particulars.

Each assertion of fact made in the particulars of the claim can be either admitted, not admitted or expressly denied and any asserted fact which is not answered by either a denial or a non-admission is deemed to have been impliedly admitted. Where a statement is made in a claim to the effect that something was not done, a simple denial is insufficient and a full statement of what actually took place should be provided. Thus the assertion contained in the example particulars of the claim shown on p 26, stating that no engineer came, should not simply be denied; instead a positive statement that the engineer did actually visit the plaintiff should be made. If the defendant does not know whether an assertion is true or not, it should be not admitted, unless the matter is entirely uncontroversial.

The particulars of the defence should be set out and numbered in a similar form to the particulars of claim. A defence to the example claim on pp 25–7 might read like this:

1. The Plaintiff's occupational status is not admitted. The Defendant was given no information by the Plaintiff in this respect.
2. It is admitted that the Plaintiff visited the Defendant's premises on 15 October 1996 and purchased two cold display cabinets. No admissions are made of any recommendations made to the Plaintiff by the Defendant.
3. It is admitted that the cabinets were delivered to the Plaintiff on 19 October 1996.
4. No admissions are made in respect of paragraph 4. of the Particulars of Claim.
5. The Defendant denies being made aware by the Plaintiff of any problem in June 1997.
6. Following a telephone call from the Plaintiff on 1 July 1997 the Defendant sent an engineer to inspect the display cabinets on 11 July 1997. No fault could be found by the engineer.
7. On 1 August 1997 the Defendant received a written request from the Plaintiff for either replacement of the cabinets or reimbursement of monies paid for them.
8. The Defendant has no record of any further communication from the Plaintiff.
9. The Defendant denies that the goods sold were not of satisfactory quality or unfit for their purpose.
10. The Defendant suggests that the Plaintiff may have misused the cabinets and that such misuse would be the sole cause of the spoiling of any food stored in them.
11. The Defendant claims costs.

Once again only an outline of the relevant facts should be included in the particulars of the defence. If the defence relies on any argument that the party making the claim has failed to mitigate the damages then the facts relevant to this must be included as well. Specific evidence such as the precise findings of the engineer on his alleged visit does not need to be included. In fact a defence can be very vague indeed and it is quite usual for it not to be readily apparent from the particulars of defence exactly how a defendant intends to defend a plaintiff's claim.

Note that where a defendant to a claim for non-payment of money pleads that the payment was offered and refused, a payment into court of the sum offered must accompany the defence if the defendant is to avoid being liable for the plaintiff's legal costs. Where such a payment is made with this defence, known as a defence of tender, the costs of the proceedings will be awarded to the defendant for work done on the case after the date of that offer, or of payment into court, provided it can be proved that the payment was actually offered.

COUNTERCLAIMS AND THIRD PARTIES

Sometimes a defendant may wish to make a claim against a plaintiff. This is called a *counterclaim* and is made by filing a *particulars of counterclaim* with the defence and completing the relevant section on the response form that accompanied the summons. The counterclaim will normally be heard at trial together with the plaintiff's claim. The procedures for a counterclaim are the same as for an ordinary claim except that, in respect of the counterclaim only, the role of the plaintiff and defendant are reversed. The defendant has to prove the counterclaim and the plaintiff disprove it. The plaintiff has the right to file a defence to the counterclaim and the pre-trial procedures for both the claim and counterclaim will run concurrently. If the counterclaim exceeds the original claim a separate court fee may be payable when it is filed with the court.

Where a defendant raises issues in the defence that on their own might constitute grounds for a counterclaim but which are instead pleaded only as a defence the plaintiff may be ordered by the court, or may sometimes voluntarily, file a *reply* to the defence which is a formal response to those issues so raised. Sometimes a defence will admit many of the facts in a particulars of claim but will assert that someone else, in other words a *third party*, has some responsibility or liability in the dispute. Where this is the case it is necessary for the defendant to file with the court a *third party notice* (Form N15) and also serve it on the third party together with a set of *particulars of the third party notice*. Damages or another remedy plus interest and costs may be sought by way of a third party notice. The third party becomes involved as a party to the proceedings and has the right to file a defence to the third party notice which will eventually be considered at trial together with the original claim.

PRE-TRIAL PROCEDURES

After the defence, any counterclaim and any third party notice have been received by the court, the case will come before a procedural judge who has the task of designating it as a *small claim* if it is worth less than £3000 (this threshold is soon to be increased to £5000); a *fast-track* case if it is for less than £10,000, with only limited procedural formalities, a fairly quick trial and a ceiling on legal costs; or, if the claim exceeds £10,000, as a *slow-track* case with full procedure and costs. Cases can be switched to a different procedure where it appears to the procedural judge that an individual case merits an alternative approach. This may often follow a request for such a change from one or more of the parties involved.

Figure 3.2 is a process chart which shows all the possible procedural steps from the service of the summons right through to trial. In the small claims and fast-track procedures certain of these steps may be left out or simplified; for example in small claims cases there is normally no pre-trial review hearing and, instead of the full disclosure of all relevant documents, the parties involved merely have to send each other copies of anything they intend to refer to at the trial. In fast-track and slow-track cases questionnaires may be sent to each party giving an opportunity to delineate the issues at the heart of the dispute.

ORIGINATING APPLICATIONS

Besides the award of damages the county courts have the power to order other remedies such as an *injunction* (an order forbidding a party from doing something), *specific performance* (whereby a party is ordered to do something), and a variety of orders relating to the ownership of property and goods. In these instances an action is commenced by an *originating application* (Form N200) instead of by summons but still follows a basically similar procedure. For the particulars, an *affidavit*, sworn on oath and stating all of the facts relevant to the case, is required. The person making the application to the court is called the *applicant* instead of the plaintiff, and the other party called the *respondent*. A typical originating application is given in Appendix 1, on pp 148–9.

It is worth noting that in certain types of case the proceedings are taken against someone who apparently has no immediate contractual link with

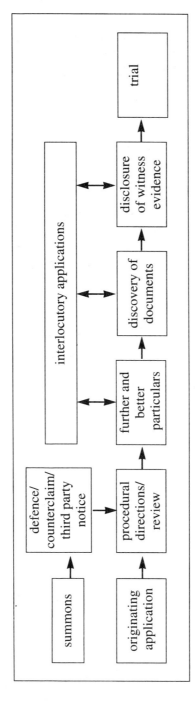

Figure 3.2 *Civil proceedings process*

the applicant or plaintiff. This phenomenon can be seen in a wide range of actions including those in respect of nuisance, negligence, copyright and statutory duty. The party against whom the proceedings are taken must always be the one who has directly caused damage to, or infringed the rights of, the applicant or plaintiff. Of course sometimes any intermediary with whom the applicant or plaintiff has had dealings would become involved as a third party or at least be called as witness.

Certain types of originating application, including most notably those made under the provisions of the Landlord and Tenant Acts, have additional procedural requirements such as the service on the respondent of a prescribed form of statutory notice prior to the filing of the application which itself must contain certain information as prescribed by statute. This information typically includes the identities of all parties involved, the precise nature of the order sought and the grounds on which the application for the order may be justified. After the service of an originating application the court will often order a review hearing for giving directions, which all of the parties involved must attend, or alternatively issue written directions for the discovery of documents and the exchange of witness statements. The matter will then proceed to a hearing in front of a judge.

THE LANDLORD AND TENANT ACTS

These Acts cover many matters relating to the renting and leasing of property. Among the categories of action which may be brought to court under the Acts are claims for compensation from a landlord for improvements made to a property by a tenant, orders compelling a landlord to carry out repairs to rented property, and matters such as the challenging of excessive service charges, the appointment of tenants as managing agents for a property, or the acquisition by the leaseholders of the freehold interest in a property. These Acts are of particular relevance where there has been unacceptable or unreasonable behaviour on the part of the landlord.

In cases where there are a number of tenants or leaseholders living in the same building it will usually be necessary for them to act together in making a joint application. A number of procedures under the Acts, such as the appointment of managing agents and freehold acquisition, require a majority of tenants to be in favour of the application and this in itself will require some form of vote. Moreover, information may have to be pooled because certain information prescribed by statute must be included in any application for it to be valid. Where a building is divided into a number of self-contained flats, and the majority of the tenants wish jointly to make a Landlord and Tenant Act application, special permission may have to be sought from the court for any single tenant (other than a practising lawyer) to represent the others in court. Evidence will normally have to be presented to support such a request. Minutes of a meeting of the tenants or a letter to the court signed by all of those wishing to be represented would probably suffice.

Proceedings may only be started after a statutory notice of specified content has been served on any other party involved or affected and this includes any third party who may, for example, be involved as mortgagee. Exceptions to this rule may arise where a landlord can no longer be traced, or where a court action for alleged arrears of rent or service charges has already been commenced. Information relating to certain criteria which must be fulfilled as to the nature of the properties in question, their occupancy, and the duration of the leases must be given. The precise requirements for the content of any relevant notice for the different categories of proceedings under the Acts can be found in *Atkin's Court Forms*, a reference book which is stocked by all good law libraries.

Following the service of the statutory notice, the action itself should be commenced by filing an originating application in the county court (or an equivalent originating summons in the High Court where applicable). Certain procedures require that there be a delay between the service of the notice and the filing of the application, of sufficient duration to enable the respondent to remedy, if possible, any breach of obligation under a lease, or any other matter, expressly cited in the notice as being the grounds for the application. Two copies of the notice must be filed with the copies of the application which itself must be of the special form prescribed in the *County Court Practice* rule book (or the *Supreme Court Practice* rule book for the High Court). If not clear from the notice or any affidavit filed in support of the application, the application must clearly state:

1. the identity of the premises (which must be at least 50 per cent residential for freehold acquisition by the tenants, the appointment of managing agents or the granting of extended leases);
2. the details of the applicants (for example, including details of the requisite majority of qualifying tenants being either 50 per cent, or in some cases two-thirds, depending on the order sought);
3. the name and address of the landlord;
4. the identity of any nominee for the management of a property or for acquiring it (this may be one person or a group of people and is not confined to persons who are leaseholders);
5. the names and addresses of all parties likely to be affected by the pro-

ceedings including all other tenants, mortgagees, etc; and

6. the grounds of the application (for example, failure to keep a building in a good state of repair, overcharging for services, harassment, etc).

The best form of presenting such information is to put it in an affidavit which could summarise all of the relevant facts including a record of any vote taken in support of the application. Without all of this information the court cannot determine whether or not all the necessary criteria are met for an order to be granted, and thus will be unable to proceed with any application. An example of an application for an order for the appointment of managing agents to a leasehold property is given in Appendix 1, pp 148–9.

DOCUMENTS FOR COURT

While certain standard forms, such as those for compiling a document list or making an application, are usually available from the court office there may be occasions where the litigant-in-person will have to produce less common standard forms for himself. Where this is the case it is important to make sure that certain requirements of the standard form are met. The first of these requirements is to identify clearly the case to which the document relates and this is the function of the document header. The header, which is illustrated in figure 3.3, includes the following elements:

1. in the top left-hand corner a statement saying in which court the case is being heard;
2. in the top right-hand corner is the case number, normally seven figures long, the first two representing the year in which the proceedings were commenced and the remaining five being the number of the case's entry on that court's register for that year;
3. in the centre of the page below this come the names of the plaintiff (or applicant), the defendant (or respondent) and any other party involved in the case.

In legal documents there is a certain protocol concerning the use of capital letters when referring to the parties, documents and the like. Wherever a noun refers to a specific entity rather than a general one it should commence with a capital letter. Thus the parties and documents in a particular case should be written as 'the Plaintiff', 'the Defendant', etc, whereas using these titles in the general sense they do not need the capitalisation.

```
IN THE _____ COUNTY COURT     CASE NO yy/xxxxx

BETWEEN


                    _____ (Plaintiff)


          and


                    _____ (Defendant)

               TITLE OF DOCUMENT

```

Figure 3.3 *Document header*

The title of the document appears below the header and simply describes what it represents, for example 'Particulars of Claim', 'Defendant's Document List', 'Third Party's Submissions' or 'The Affidavit of N. E. Body'. This title should be printed boldly and in capitals with, conventionally, lines above and below, so that the title stands out. The text of the document may then start just below the title or it may start on the next page. Standard texts for certain court documents can be found listed in the *County Court Practice* rule book, and these should be used wherever applicable.

Affidavits, which are signed statements of fact, should be written in the first person only and an oath sworn at the time of signing which must be witnessed by either a court official or a solicitor. A copy of each document referred to in an affidavit must be attached and endorsed with the words 'This is the document herein referred to as A' (or B, C, D, etc for each subsequent document mentioned) and cross-referenced as such within the affidavit text.

FURTHER AND BETTER PARTICULARS

In more complex cases the parties to court proceedings will often request from each other *further and better particulars* of the claim, defence, counterclaim or third party notice. Obtaining more detailed particulars has the advantage of allowing the facts which are in dispute to be more clearly delineated. The method of requesting further and better particulars is the same for both the plaintiff and defendant and relatively straightforward. A series of numbered questions are simply listed under the standard header and, as well as sending a copy to the other party, a copy should be sent to the court to go on record there. A reply to the questions should be received within 14 days of the other party receiving the request. If no response is forthcoming you will have to make an *application* to the court (a procedure which is explained on pp 48–49 below).

When making a request for further and better particulars great care should be taken with the wording so as not to inadvertently admit any allegation in the other parties particulars which you seek to deny. For example, to continue from our example on pp 25–7, the following questions might be asked:

1. In respect of paragraph 3 of the Particulars of Claim please state exactly what recommendation was alleged to have been made, stating when, in what manner and by whom it was allegedly made.
2. In respect of paragraph 9 of the Particulars of Claim please state what alleged defects rendered the goods not of satisfactory quality or unfit for the purpose for which they were sold.

The further and better particulars, together with the original particulars, form what is known as a party's *pleadings* and must include all material facts on which their case relies. Use the request for further and better particulars to probe the other party's case. Look for weaknesses in their version of events and concentrate on any facts that they allege which you feel are not correct. Applications may be made to the court in slow track cases for a party's pleadings to be *struck out* where there is an unreasonable failure to provide further and better particulars.

AMENDMENTS TO PLEADINGS

It may happen, because of a mistake or error, that a party may wish to make an amendment to their pleadings or other court documents. An amendment to pleadings may be made at any time up until the close of pleadings, that is up until the filing of a defence or of further and better particulars if there are any. A copy of the amended pleading should be filed with the court and served on all other parties. It must be clearly marked 'Amended Particulars of Claim' or 'Amended Defence', etc and all changes from the original should be underlined, preferably with a red pen.

After the close of pleadings such an amendment will only be allowed with the *leave* or permission of the court. An application on notice is necessary to obtain such leave and grounds will have to be given for the necessity of the changes. A typical reason might be that new evidence had just come to light during the discovery stage of proceedings. Where a significant amendment is made to a particulars of claim the court will frequently grant leave for the defence also to be amended to take account of the changes.

Amendments to other documents such as document lists or notices of application should simply be filed with the court and served on the other parties as soon as possible after it is realised it is necessary. An amendment to an important document may constitute sufficient grounds for the adjournment of a forthcoming hearing if insufficient notice of the change is given.

PAYMENT INTO COURT

At any time before the final judgement is delivered in a case money can be paid into court in respect of any claim including counterclaims and third party notices. If the full amount of damages claimed, plus all costs accrued up to the time of paying it in, is paid into court, then the party making the claim is obliged to accept the money and withdraw the proceedings. A lesser amount may be paid into court and when this is done the other party must decide whether or not to accept the payment in full and final settlement of the claim. When such a lesser amount is paid into court the party paying it in should take care to make sure that it is clear to the court and to the other party whether or not it includes the costs as well as the damages. When a lesser sum has been paid in and is not accepted by the other party then that money stays in court until after judgement is delivered. More than one payment into court can be made by any party and, as will be explained on p 69, payment into court can affect the award of costs to the successful party.

Payments into court should be made out to HMPG and be accompanied by a letter fully explaining what the payment is made in respect of. As with all communications to the court the case number and the names of the parties should be clearly given. If there has been a payment into court in a case, under no circumstances should this payment be mentioned to the trial judge until after he has decided the case.

SUMMARY JUDGEMENT AND STRIKING-OUT

As well as by means of a payment being made into court, there are a number of ways in which a case can be decided without actually going to trial. An early summary judgement can be entered in favour of a plaintiff's claim or a party's pleadings struck out, which has the effect of preventing them from proceeding with their claim or defence. These procedures for determining a case are only employed sparingly because in general the court will always prefer the option of a full hearing of the matter as that is seen as being more fair and just. The threat of summary judgement and striking out are, however, very important as a means of ensuring compliance with pre-trial procedures.

Summary judgement can be entered where no defence, or notice of intention to defend a case, has been delivered to the court within the prescribed period. It can also be entered where a claim or particularly a defence can be shown to have no real substance and thus has no chance of success. An application for summary judgement on these grounds will be heard by the district judge and both sides will have the chance to argue their position. Unless the matter is really clear-cut then the judge will normally dismiss the application for summary judgement and order that the case proceed to trial in the normal manner.

The district judge will also hear any interlocutory application for a claim or a defence to be struck out. The grounds for striking out pleadings normally relate to the failure of a party to carry out an order of court to serve further and better particulars, document lists, copy documents and the like. There are also, however, provisions in the court rules for claims to be struck out on the grounds that they are malicious, frivolous, scandalous or otherwise an abuse of the court process. Again the application will normally be heard on notice and each side will have the opportunity to justify its position. The benefit of any doubt will always be given so as to allow the proceedings to continue on their normal course to trial. Any summary judgement or striking-out can be appealed against.

SETTLING OUT OF COURT

During the course of court proceedings one of the parties may make overtures to the other with a view to agreeing a compromise solution. It is always much cheaper to settle any dispute early on before the legal costs of each side become too much of a significant factor. When making any offer to settle out of court it is customary to write 'Without Prejudice' above the text of the offer. Letters marked with these words are not normally allowed to be put before the judge as they may unduly influence his appraisal of a case.

When deciding whether or not to settle a case out of court reference should always be made to the likely outcome out of trial. Generally a defendant will offer somewhat less than the full amount claimed and will be prepared to barter with the other side. An offer to settle can be made at any time during court proceedings and may particularly take place after the disclosure of documentary and witness evidence when the strength or otherwise of the plaintiff's and defendant's cases becomes more apparent. Any offer of settlement may include specific terms such as the plaintiff agreeing not to talk publicly about the matter as well as more general terms which deny any liability on the part of the defendant. Once agreed, the exact terms of the settlement should be embodied in writing and signed by each party. Only after any monies due under the settlement are paid should a standard notice formally withdrawing the action be delivered to the court. A properly agreed settlement can be the basis of a subsequent new court action if the terms are not kept.

Beware, an offer of settlement may sometimes be made as a delaying tactic, a party defending a claim may appear willing to open negotiations in return for the adjournment of a hearing. Do not fall into this trap: someone making this sort of offer is only playing for time. Use the impending hearing as a negotiating tool to bring about a speedy resolution to the case. Remember that the court rules allow for a claim to be struck out if it is not set down (ie scheduled) for trial within 15 months of the start of the court proceedings.

THE DISCLOSURE OF DOCUMENTS

Some time after the court has received a defence, *directions* will be given concerning the *disclosure* or *discovery* of the evidence to be given at trial. Usually this is a timetable consisting of matters that should be done and time limits for doing them. In most cases these directions will simply be posted to each of the parties. Occasionally they will be given in person by a judge at a *pre-trial review* hearing (also called a *preliminary appointment* in small claims) or at an application hearing.

The first stage of discovery usually takes place some four to six weeks from the date when the directions are given. Each party must send to the other a list of all documents they hold relating to the case. Certain types of document, for example communications between a party and his legal advisor, should be listed as 'privileged' documents which do not have to be shown to the other party. On receipt of these lists each party has 7 or 14 days within which to request copies of the other's documents. These copies should then be sent within the period ordered in the directions. One is allowed to charge a reasonable copying fee to the party requesting the documents, but in practice where similar numbers of copy documents are required by each party no fee is generally required. Sometimes the directions will simply order each side to send the other copies of any documents and witness statements which they intend to present as evidence before the court.

The procedures for discovery leave plenty of scope for delaying tactics with the usual excuse being that as there are so many documents it will take a long time to find them all. Making an application on notice will remedy the situation but do give the other side a few extra days after the deadline to allow for postal and other genuine delays. Once again precise details of the rules regarding discovery, applications and all other aspects of this procedure can be found in the *County Court Practice* rule book which can be found in many public libraries.

WITNESS EVIDENCE

After the exchange of copy documents the next step is to disclose witness evidence, of which there are two categories: ordinary *witnesses*, who can testify as to the true facts of the matter; and *expert witnesses* who can give expert technical opinions based on those facts. Because it is important where possible to corroborate your version of events with the testimony of independent witnesses you should try to talk to any person who has knowledge of the subject matter of your case. Find out exactly what they have to say about the situation and consider whether it could help you. You should also write to the other party or their solicitors asking what witness evidence they intend to produce at trial.

If there are any expert witnesses, a report or summary of their opinion evidence should be sent to all other parties. Remember that at the trial a written report may not be sufficient: the other side may question the validity of the report and they have the right to cross-examine any witness who has prepared a report.

Despite the fact that they have the right to be compensated for their time in court, people are sometimes reluctant to agree to act as a witness in court and it may be necessary to serve a witness summons to compel someone to attend the trial. In small claims and fast-track cases a written witness statement or an affidavit will usually suffice, but in a slow-track case, if you are not 100 per cent sure that a particular witness will show up voluntarily for the hearing you should obtain a witness summons for them. The procedure is quite simple: you should go to the court office, fill out the relevant form and pay a court fee which includes two elements, travelling and subsistence allowances for the witness (the court will tell you the minimum you have to offer to pay for this) and a bailiff's fee for serving the summons on the witness. You can serve a witness summons personally yourself as long you swear an affidavit of service at the court office straight away after you have done so.

Witness statements should be signed and dated by the witness with an attestation confirming that statement is true and is in the witness's own words.

As well as witness evidence one can present physical evidence at a trial. Typical examples of physical evidence are faulty or broken goods which can be produced for the inspection of the judge. Normally the party in possession of these goods should allow inspection by the opposition well ahead of the trial if requested. If the goods are too large or heavy to bring to the court the judge will, if he thinks fit, arrange an inspection visit accompanied by the two parties.

NOTICES TO ADMIT FACTS OR DOCUMENTS

At any time during the proceedings, even immediately after the pleadings but more usually after the disclosure of evidence, one party may require the other to expressly admit various facts relating to the case. This is done by serving a *Notice to Admit Facts* listing the precise facts in question. The party receiving the notice must then reply within the next seven days stating whether each fact is expressly admitted or not admitted. Any facts that are admitted no longer have to be proved by presenting evidence at trial and the party making the admission no longer has the right to contest these facts. If no reply is sent then the facts are deemed to have been admitted and it is possible that the party who sent the notice could apply for summary judgement on the grounds that the admission shows the other side to have no real case.

The notice to admit can also be a good way of making the opposition realise how weak their case is and this can be a useful tool to help bring about a serious offer to settle out of court. It can also serve to focus attention on the real issues that have to be settled by the evidence. If a number of facts are admitted then the trial can be somewhat simplified although there still remains the problem of how the law should be applied to these facts.

Similar in application is the *Notice to Admit Documents* which as the name suggests requires the party receiving it to admit the authenticity and contents of certain listed documents. Again if no reply is served then the documents are deemed to have been admitted. Getting the opposition to admit documents can avoid the necessity of calling the authors of the documents to attend court as witnesses. Remember that although the authenticity and contents may be admitted there still remains the question of the interpretation of those contents.

THE CIVIL EVIDENCE ACTS

There are certain types of evidence which, if they are to be presented in court during civil proceedings, must be preceded by a special notice that must be served on all other parties in the case. Such evidence, which may fall across more than one category, includes:

1. any statement, in whatever form, made by anyone with knowledge of the facts of a case such as would make them eligible as a witness, regardless of whether or not there is any intention to actually call them to give direct testimony before the court (under section 2 of the Act);
2. any record, such as a customer services file or a transcript of a meeting (under section 4 of the Act);
3. any computer-produced document such as a statement of account or a standard letter (under section 5 of the Act).

Where it is intended that such evidence is to be presented before the court, a formal notice must be served within 21 days of the matter being set down for trial. The notice must contain:

1. Details of any statement including:
   - the time, the place and the circumstances in which it was made;
   - the identity of the persons by whom and to whom it was made; and
   - the substance of the statement, where relevant using the precise words, or
   - if applicable, a copy of the document in which the statement was made.
2. Details of any record including:
   - those of the person who compiled the record;
   - those of each and every person who supplied the information from which the record was compiled; and
   - those of any other person through whom that information was supplied.
3. Details of any computer-generated document including:
   - those of a person who was responsible for the management of the functioning of the computer during any relevant period;
   - those of a person who was responsible for the supply of relevant information to the computer; and
   - those of a person who was responsible for the operation of the computer during any relevant period.

The notice should also state whether the computer was functioning properly throughout any relevant period, and must note any time when the functioning was such that the production of the document or the accuracy of its contents would have been affected. If any person named in the notice is unavailable to attend any trial or hearing as a witness the notice must specify this and state the reason why. Sometimes a party will seek to gain advantage by failing to include all of the necessary information. If you receive such a defective notice you should write immediately to the sender asking for the missing items of information.

Upon receipt of a Civil Evidence Act notice, the receiver of the notice may serve a counter-notice on the sender. This counter-notice can require the party who issued the original notice to call as a witness any person or persons named in it. The non-availability of any witness may also be challenged with a counter-notice by requiring that they should be called. In this instance evidence will have to be put before the court as proof of non-availability if the witness does not attend. Failure to comply with the requirements of a counter-notice may render the relevant evidence inadmissible in court, although, as always, the judge has a very wide discretion in what to allow or disallow.

The manner of presentation before the court of any statement that is covered by the Act is also prescribed. In practice this generally means that where the person who made a statement appears in court as a witness, the statement itself should not be put in evidence without the permission of the judge and, if allowed, should not normally be presented before the examination-in-chief of that witness is complete. This rule is to prevent, as far as possible, the testimony of the witness from being prejudiced, biased, limited or otherwise affected by any previous mention of the statement during the hearing.

DELAYING TACTICS

As a litigant-in-person you should be aware that from time to time some parties involved in court proceedings may try to obtain advantage by employing somewhat unscrupulous tactics to delay the course of justice. This is just as true where solicitors are involved as it is in cases fought solely between litigants-in-person. Some of the most common problems you may encounter are described below.

By far the most common form of delaying tactic is for the defendant to pretend that he did not receive the initial court summons. Where this is the case the defendant will normally do nothing until the plaintiff commences enforcement proceedings after obtaining summary judgement. At this point the defendant will say he knew nothing at all about the court action. Several weeks' worth of time and effort by the plaintiff will have been wasted and the whole court procedure will have to be recommenced by re-serving the summons. Delivery of an additional copy of the original summons by hand or by recorded delivery post will usually defeat this tactic. Note that there are some people who will refuse to accept anything sent by recorded delivery post in which case service by hand is the only option. An affidavit of service should be sworn at the court office immediately after the copy has been delivered (or posted by recorded delivery) to verify the facts of the service of the document.

The documents which receive the evasive treatment are by no means limited to summonses. Practically every type of document imaginable is susceptible to the age old adage 'it must have got lost in the post'. In my experience a few, but very, very few things that are posted fail to arrive but what does that matter? Again delivery by hand or recorded delivery post usually remedies the problem, although even then it will sometimes be claimed that the documents did not get through to the right person. In an extreme case these problems can be overcome by handing the necessary documents to the representative of the other party at a court hearing for summary judgement or any other hearing. Note the court will generally give the benefit of the doubt to anyone claiming to have not received a document and will order the document to be served again and that stage of the procedure recommenced.

Another common delaying tactic is for a party to fail to send documents to the other party on time. Indeed some parties only appear willing to comply with the court's orders for the discovery and disclosure of documents when faced with an application for their pleadings to be struck out on the grounds of particular documents not being sent. Therefore do not wait too long after any deadline to make an application in this respect; you will probably have to wait two or three months for the hearing of the application and you will be unlikely to receive the lacking documents much before then.

Delays caused by the failure to send out necessary documents are very common, very repetitious and often account for the long-drawn-out nature of the more important civil cases. It is one of the ironies of the legal system that many defendants faced with a case they fear they might lose run up large legal costs for themselves by employing exhausting delaying games rather than cutting their losses and settling the case early.

A further problem is for documents to be sent but wrongly addressed. Though less common this tactic, rather than simply delaying the proceedings, can even in some extreme cases influence the outcome of the case. Expert witness statements and other late disclosures of evidence miraculously lose their way in the post because of a chance typing error in the address. At trial this evidence is usually admitted even though one side has been taken totally by surprise because of the 'accidental' slip. It is astonishing that this trick succeeds even when a copy clearly displaying the 'mistake' has been put before the judge.

There are two ways of countering this ploy, the first being simply to write to the other side once a date has been set for trial asking them to confirm that they have no further evidence beyond that which you have received. You should list the evidence you have received to avoid any confusion. It is possible that they may deliberately lie to you in their reply but if they do then at least you will have better grounds for demanding an adjournment at trial if the last-minute evidence trick is pulled. You should ask for the costs of the adjournment 'in any event' as it has been made necessary only because of the mistakes or errors of the other party.

Unfortunately beyond these examples of gamesmanship there are more serious dirty tricks that are sometimes encountered by the litigant-in-person. These include the use of evidence which has been fabricated solely for use during the court proceedings. This problem is so widespread there is even a polite name for it: *manufactured* evidence. All sorts of things come into this category: letters which were never written before the matter got to court; falsified accounts or computer records; and even the misleading written statements of witnesses. The purpose of such false evidence is clear: to unduly influence the outcome of a case and because of its doubtful nature it is often only disclosed to the opposition very late; just before trial. This sort of tactic is very difficult to combat because ultimately it brings the trial down to the level of one person's true word against another's lies.

Only very thorough preparatory work before the trial can defeat false evidence. The exact counter-measures required must of course depend on the type of evidence itself. In the case of a letter you will have to go back to correspondence that actually took place: can you show that the letter is out of style or out of chronological order with other letters which were actually written? Sometimes there will be a file reference number that can be checked. Are there any other letters or documents which in any way contradict or are inconsistent with the false evidence? Remember the judge does not know what evidence to believe: you must prove your version of the facts to him.

In the case of falsified accounts or computer records you will have to analyse them item by item, date by date. Compile your own account or record: it might make the problem easier to understand. You will have to produce documents that show some degree of corroboration of your evidence such as bank statements and correspondence with other interested parties. Remember that you should, if you can, call witnesses to support these documents and if this is not possible you should serve a notice to admit or a notice under the Civil Evidence Act as applicable. You should insist on the author of any dubious letter, or the person responsible for compiling the false account or computer record, being available as a witness for the trial. Don't be frightened to serve a witness summons to force someone to attend trial if you think it will help your cause. Prepare very thorough questions for any witnesses to draw out and play on any inconsistencies or uncertainties in their evidence. You may have to improvise a bit at trial to make further capital of any weaknesses that can be found by your initial questioning. Well-ordered notes will assist greatly in this.

In the face of a witness statement that appears to be false, you should always make sure that you will be able to question that witness in open court in front of the judge. That way the person's evidence cannot come before the court without them being available for cross-examination. When questioned in person it is far more difficult for someone to lie convincingly than when simply signing a statement that someone else has prepared. Again you could consider serving a witness summons and again carefully prepare questions that will be difficult for them to answer.

Try to surprise them with an oblique line of questioning. Play on any hesitation they may show by saying 'you don't sound too sure' or similar as this will greatly increase the pressure on them to tell the truth. Bear in mind that if at trial you call a witness yourself who is not co-operative you will have to ask the judge to allow you to treat them as 'hostile', which means that you may examine them more in the manner of a cross-examination than is normally allowed. This would allow you to ask leading questions which will make your task easier. However, only witnesses who are very reticent or unhelpful can ever be treated in this way by the party that has called them. Beware that if you call one of the other side's witnesses they may still give false evidence which will go very much against you. After all there is a chance that the witness may not really intend to give evidence for the opposition anyway.

Make sure that you can present as much evidence as possible to contradict any false evidence that might be presented by the other side; if you cannot, the false evidence may even be accepted by default. Do not expect the truth to be understood by the judge without you being able to fully explain all of the facts. He will know nothing about the case other than what you and the opposition tell him. You will have to make him understand and without leaving any room for doubt.

The research for this book gave me the opportunity to note at first hand the impeccable delaying tactics of one Cambridge-educated barrister defending a case on behalf of a household name. He managed to keep the case going nine months without even getting beyond the pleadings. The other side had the last laugh because, when the claim was settled out of court, the barrister's clients had to pay a further 600 per cent on top for the other side's legal costs. There's a moral in there somewhere.

APPLICATIONS

In the face of obstructive tactics on the part of the opposition it is frequently necessary to make an *application for an interlocutory order*, in other words to apply for a court order compelling the other party to do something. This, for example, may be to compel them to disclose documents, or to agree to a date being set for trial. There are countless occasions when an application may be necessary to prevent the proceedings from grinding to an absolute halt.

Applications fall into two categories: applications *on notice* and *ex parte* applications. Normally applications will be made on written notice to the other party or parties, allowing them the right to attend a hearing to contest the application. An application will normally be heard at the next hearing if one has already been scheduled. If not, a new hearing for the application will be arranged, usually for two or three months later, at which the parties may present limited evidence and argue their position in person before a district judge.

Ex parte applications are normally only allowed in a matter of some urgency or where the other party has continued to disregard the rules of court. An *ex parte* application, where allowed, can usually be made simply by writing a letter, or better still swearing an affidavit, containing the relevant facts and marking it for the attention of the district judge care of the Chief Clerk of the court.

There is a standard form for making an application on notice, Form N244 called a *Notice of an Application*, which can be obtained from the court office. It is necessary to fill out three copies (four if there is a third party), one for each party and one for the court. The nature of the order and the grounds on which it is being sought should be clearly stated. If there is more than one order being sought then number each point for clarity. It is advisable to always include claim for 'costs in any event' in the application. There is a court fee for making an interlocutory application. All of the copies are filed with the court who will arrange a time for a hearing and send a copy to each party. If there are any dates when it would not be possible for you to attend court, for example because you will be on holiday, let the court know when you hand in or send in the application forms.

Once again it is common for parties to pretend that they have not received a copy of an application so it is worth sending an additional copy by hand, by recorded delivery or by fax. In many instances the problem which gave rise to the necessity of the application is remedied in the final week or so before the application is due to be heard. In such instances it is best to notify the court and officially withdraw the application.

SCHEDULING HEARINGS

Despite the fact that dates for all hearings are supposed to be automatically scheduled by the court, very often it will be necessary to communicate with the court office to make sure that a hearing is fixed, more especially if you wish to ensure that it is set for a convenient date and time. If there are any dates on which you will be unavailable for a hearing you should let the court know before the hearing is scheduled. It is usually possible to talk directly to the listings clerk who can then take account of these unavailable dates. If you are taken by surprise and a hearing is scheduled when you did not expect it then you should contact the court immediately you receive notice of that hearing and ask for it to be rescheduled. Any delay in making the request for rescheduling will make it less likely that the request will be met with agreement. If possible you should obtain the written consent of all other parties because this will virtually guarantee the granting of an adjournment and the rescheduling of the hearing.

Note that the procedure for scheduling a trial can be slightly different in so much that the court will usually require all parties to have completed a *certificate of readiness* for the trial. This certificate has spaces for each party to list any dates for which they are unavailable to attend court and also requires them to state how long they expect the trial to last. It is always very difficult even for professionals to estimate the length of a trial as they can be unpredictable affairs. Try to calculate how long it would take for all the witnesses to give their evidence and then treble it to allow for the judge's note-taking and any legal arguments. That should give you a rough idea.

A blank certificate can be obtained from the court office by any party who will then fill in their part and send it on to the other party or parties to do likewise and then return it to the court. If the certificate is not returned to the court within a reasonable time, such as 14 days per party, then it will be necessary for one of the parties to make an application to have a date set for the trial. A party who fails to complete a certificate of readiness without good reason will usually have to pay the costs of such an application and may also find it very difficult to get the trial rescheduled even when the date is inconvenient for their witnesses. Failing to fill in the certificate of readiness can therefore possibly have serious repercussions that may even affect the outcome of the case.

THE APPLICATION HEARING

The hearing of an application is relatively informal and is heard privately in *chambers* not in open court. Although there is no strict dress code you should dress smartly. Remember that the judge is only human and therefore his first impressions of you will depend very much on the way you look. Bear in mind that it can be decidedly cold in some older courthouses in the depths of winter.

You have the right to have someone, such as a friend, a colleague or a union representative, accompany you to any court hearing including trials and arbitrations to lend advice and moral support. A non-professional who accompanies a litigant-in-person is called a *McKenzie friend* after the case in which this right was established. With the permission of the court, the Mckenzie friend may also address the court on behalf of the litigant-in-person. Note, however, that the McKenzie friend must accompany the litigant to court and cannot attend the hearing in his place; only a solicitor or barrister has that right.

The hearing will probably take place somewhat later than the time originally notified as the scheduled time is when the district judge will start working through a whole list of minor hearings booked for that session. However, it would be extremely foolish to arrive any later than that time. On arrival at the court find out which room your hearing will take place in; there will be some lists displaying this information. If in any doubt ask one of the court ushers (who are recognisable by their blackgowns) or even the security guard who will give you directions. When you have located the courtroom for your hearing wait outside until an usher appears. The usher will take down the names of everyone present for the hearings and call the cases into the courtroom when the district judge is ready for them.

The hearing of an application normally only lasts a few minutes and should you need to speak to the judge he or she should be addressed as 'Your Honour'. Each party in turn may be asked to justify their position in relation to the application, although in practice the judge will have often already made his mind up what to do from reading the notice of the application. If any party does not turn up it is likely that the Judge will decide the application and award costs against them. If any party is represented by solicitors who are based some distance away from the court they will probably appoint a local solicitor as an agent to attend the hearing on their behalf. If there is someone from the opposition present it is always worth trying to negotiate an agreed settlement. In any event the outcome of the application may be contested by making an appeal to a more senior judge.

PREPARING FOR TRIAL

Once each side has disclosed its evidence it is time to make final preparations for the trial. Scrutinise the evidence very closely and ask yourself the following questions:

1. Is there enough evidence to support your side of the argument? To succeed you must prove every relevant fact.

2. If there is not enough evidence then decide what is lacking and remedy this deficiency.
3. How are the opposition going to answer this evidence? They are bound to question your credibility as a witness. They may also have their own very different interpretation of that evidence. Is there any proof as to how the evidence should be properly interpreted?
4. What is the evidence which contradicts your argument? How are you going to answer that evidence? Can you find a way of interpreting it in your favour?
5. Can you find any weaknesses in your opponent's evidence? Are there any mistakes, inaccuracies or inconsistencies in the evidence? Could some of the documents have been 'manufactured' just for the court case? Make further enquiries if you have to.

Try to see the evidence from the judge's impartial point of view: he is the person who must be convinced that you are in the right. Go through every distinct fact which is in dispute in the pleadings. Compare the evidence for and against each one. Never forget that most evidence can be interpreted in a number of ways. Compile a list if it helps, it may prove a useful source of reference at trial. Think up and commit to paper questions for each of the witnesses, your own witnesses first and then probing questions for those on the other side. The precise nature of the questions must of course depend on the individual case but ought to become apparent by working back from the facts which have to be proved. Only when you are sure you understand all of the evidence should you move on to the legal arguments.

The legal considerations of any case are twofold: taking precedence, of course, is the question of the law as it stands in relation to the proceedings; but there is also the question of what is a just or unjust remedy to the situation. On occasion the law can be decidedly unjust if applied to its very letter; hence the need for an interpretation of the law tempered by the needs of justice. But everybody has their own idea of justice so the law must always prevail.

It is understanding and arguing the questions of law which will undoubtedly be the most difficult task for a litigant-in-person. There can be no substitute for a thorough reading of the law as it relates to the individual case. It may well be that one has to answer informed legal reasoning of a barrister and that simply cannot be done without knowing what the law is. Fortunately it is not impossible to gain this knowledge in a short period of time. The first step is to find a specialist text covering the particular area of law that relates to the subject matter of the case. Finding such a book is not always easy so I have listed a few suggestions in Appendix 4, p 167.

Once you have found a useful book, make photocopies of the relevant passages; they will be useful to quote at trial. Although in principle only practitioners' books (ie, those specially written for practising lawyers) are quotable in court, a photocopy from any law book will help add weight to your argument. If there is a fairly large sum of money at stake, anything over £3000, then it is quite possible that you will have to face a barrister. If so you will have to delve deeper.

Go to the statutes and cited cases; again copy any relevant passages. Try to grasp the underlying legal principle involved in your case. Use a highlighter pen to mark anything that may be worth quoting. Try to anticipate how the opposition will argue their position. It is not easy; it is hard work, and you get nothing for almost winning a case. If you lose you will almost certainly have to pay the other side's costs which may well exceed any damages claimed. So persevere; the law is not the mystery that it is made out to be; it *is* something the ordinary person can understand.

Make time during your preparatory work to visit your local courthouse and sit in on a trial. The court ushers will be able to tell you cases you can spectate on and may be able to suggest a case similar to yours. Get there early enough so as not to miss the start. The proceedings will be quite easy to follow. Try to understand how the judge decides the various issues and arrives at a final judgement. Imagine what it will be like to give evidence and to argue a case yourself. Rest assured the courtroom is not as daunting as one might at first think.

It is best that you plan to finish your main preparation at least a week or two before the trial date. This should then leave enough time for working on the presentation of your case. As well as committing to memory as much of the subject matter of the case as you can, you should also prepare reference material for the trial. Bundles of copies of all the relevant documents should be put together in date order. Make one bundle for each party plus one for the judge. Provide a list of contents on the front for ease of use.

Collate your notes on the evidence. Finalise your questions for the witnesses and write them down. Use a separate sheet of paper for each witness and don't forget to leave enough space to note down their answers. Remember that you will also need to make notes on the opposition's evidence so make sure you have plenty of paper and some reliable pens. A choice of coloured pens can be advantageous so that you can make further notes on your original notes without getting confused. Using a red pen or a highlighter will help make the important points more easy to find. Draft a speech outlining your legal arguments and collate this and any photocopies of statutes and case law into the document bundles.

Don't worry about the cost of all this because it will be covered by your costs when you win your case. If you don't think you are going to win your case, last-minute anxieties aside, then you should have already made a serious offer to settle with the other party. That way at least you might be able to avoid the extra cost of a day in court.

Finally a few days before the hearing you should check any travelling arrangements, decide what you are going to wear and prepare any physical evidence which needs to be produced at the trial. Plan to arrive at the courthouse at the very least half an hour before the start of the hearing and make allowances for any possible travel delays.

Be warned that sometimes the other party may make last-minute amendments to the pleadings and disclose further documents that have supposedly turned up just at the last moment. Be prepared to rethink your strategy. If the documents have changed the whole complexion of the case you should make an application either to have the documents ruled inadmissible on the grounds of late discovery or alternatively to ask for an adjournment on the same grounds. If this is necessary don't forget to ask for the costs of the application and the wasted day 'in any event'. A late application of this sort will most probably be heard at the time the trial was supposed to begin. Be prepared to continue with the trial once the application has been heard should your application for an adjournment be turned down.

- Receive full set of documents and witness statements
- Sort evidence into favourable/unfavourable/ambiguous
- Prepare notes on interpreting evidence
- Prepare notes on the legal basis of your case
- Prepare photocopies of documentary evidence
- Prepare photocopies of law books, law reports, etc
- Prepare notes for questioning witnesses
- Prepare counter-arguments against opposition case
- Inform witnesses of hearing, obtain witness summons, etc
- Check location of court, make travel arrangements

Figure 3.4 *Trial checklist*

HOW TO PREPARE LEGAL ARGUMENTS

No matter what the circumstances were that caused you to become involved in court proceedings, you must understand that the judge is obliged to follow the established principles of the law to decide the rights, wrongs and remedies of any situation. In order to have any chance of success in court you must therefore have at least a rough grasp of these principles yourself. To be totally sure of success you must be able to put legal arguments across to the judge that are both coherent and convincing. This is not a simple task. Barristers undertake years of special training and study to perfect their skills in this area. You must be prepared to put in at least a few hours of work in this respect. In order to help formulate your own legal arguments you may like to follow the 20 steps listed below.

1. List each and every fact asserted in the particulars of the claim.
2. Do likewise for the defence and, if applicable, the third party notice and defence.
3. List every difference between these lists of asserted facts.
4. List the evidence that can be brought before the court by each side to prove or disprove each of the differences of asserted facts.
5. Consult a specialised text covering the field of law that relates to your case. Sometimes there will be more than one area of the law that is relevant. *Halsbury's Laws of England* and its supplements is usually a good starter; otherwise try some of the titles included in Appendix 4, p 167. The staff at any library with a good law collection may also be able to recommend useful titles.
6. Start your search in the index and look for any sections that might relate to your case. As soon as you find anything relevant note down the general point of law and the law report or statutory reference which embodies that principle of law. Take photocopies of any passages that seem to justify your case; in court these can be put before the judge to help make your point. Use a highlighter pen to draw attention to the relevant parts of the text.
7. Before you put the book down, flick through its pages to see if there are any other points of law that may be important. If you have the time, read the whole book or at least the whole chapters that concern you.
8. Repeat steps 5, 6 and 7 with any other relevant books you can find.
9. If in court you are likely to be faced by a barrister or experienced solicitor it is probably worth your going a bit further and consulting the law reports of the actual cases and statutes you have found. Again take photocopies of these and highlight the most important passages.

10. If you get time then go on to the law reports and statutes mentioned in these.
11. Compare the facts and the evidence you have listed with the various points of law you have found.
12. List the legal principles in your favour together with their references.
13. List those not in your favour.
14. Make a special note of any legal principles that allow for a negative interpretation of your own asserted facts.
15. Write a paragraph on each of the differences of fact listed in step 3 above. Summarise the facts in issue and say why they should be decided in line with your interpretation. Outline the principles of law involved and quote its reference.
16. On separate paper do the same for the legal principles listed in step 14 above.
17. From this try to foresee how the opposition will try to argue their case and prepare at least an outline response to that line of argument. There is nothing to prevent you from delivering a written answer to the opposition's legal arguments if you are fairly sure what these may be.
18. Consider the principle of mitigation as it applies to your case (see pp 67–8).
19. If relevant, write a paragraph summarising your position with regards to mitigation.
20. Close your legal arguments with an overall summary justifying the judge's decision in your favour.

When preparing legal arguments, never forget that the more there is at stake in a case, the more hard fought it will be, and therefore the more intense the legal argument. Above all be thorough and attempt to cover all possible angles. Always prepare a written document of submissions containing your legal argument, you will be allowed to read directly from this during the trial.

SMALL CLAIMS HEARINGS

Almost all claims for less than £3000 and certain other larger claims are dealt with by arbitration (as the small claims court 'hearing' is known) instead of trial. Any larger claim may be referred to arbitration if all of the parties agree to it. There is a space on both the application for a summons and the reply form where either party can request arbitration proceedings. An arbitration hearing is much less formal than a full trial and is held in private. Solicitors' fees are generally excluded from any award of arbitration costs giving people a incentive to represent themselves; though for the same reason, a party which uses a solicitor will be unlikely to agree to arbitration if they don't have to. Pre-hearing procedures are more streamlined with each party simply required to send to the other copies of the documents they intend to produce as evidence. The hearing too is less structured than a full trial with the judge unencumbered by strict rules of procedure.

The hearing begins with the district judge reading through the particulars of claim and the defence. Once he understands the dispute he will begin to ask about the situation in greater detail. The party bearing the burden of having to prove their case will generally put their side of the case first; this will usually be the plaintiff, the person making the claim. After they have finished, the defendant will be asked to give his version of events. The presentation of witnesses will be largely under the control of the judge and his permission should be asked if you would like a particular witness to be called.

The judge will be making notes for his own reference throughout the hearing so don't speak too quickly. Start from the very beginning and describe events in the order in which they took place. Wherever necessary refer to the evidence you have brought with you. Pause now and then as necessary for the judge to catch up with his note-taking. If you think he might have missed an important point, repeat it. He should respectfully be addressed 'Your Honour'; and remember he is independent, he is there to see that justice is done. If you feel you are not getting a proper say don't get angry or shout at him. Don't interrupt unless it is absolutely crucial; if you do have to cut in do so politely and apologetically. You are entitled to your say but be patient if you have to wait to have it. Being aggressive will achieve nothing and behaving that way may only convince the judge that you are the sort of person who causes confrontations and disputes.

In an arbitration hearing the judge has a discretion to call the witnesses in any order he thinks appropriate. The witnesses brought by the parties will normally be questioned by the judge either immediately after the party bringing them has given evidence or quite commonly after the judge has heard evidence from both parties. Although each party may not be invited to directly question the witnesses, the judge will listen to suggestions for fair questions from any party.

When he feels he has a proper understanding of the situation the judge may ask the parties how they feel about possible remedies to the dispute. He will usually openly welcome any realistic propositions for a solution. If at all possible he will try to guide the parties to an agreed compromise settlement. If not, he will give his opinion of the rights and wrongs of either party's behaviour. Ultimately he has the final say and may award limited costs to the successful party as long as in his opinion they have acted reasonably and have not been in some way responsible for causing the dispute.

Note that there is normally no appeal from arbitration decisions although if for some reason something goes completely wrong a decision can be set aside on application as long it is not an agreed settlement. An agreed settlement cannot be varied once made. An arbitration judgement can be enforced in the same ways as a judgement delivered in a full county court trial.

CONVINCING THE JUDGE

A number of different factors are important in getting your message across the courtroom to the judge. In order to maximise your chances of success you should pay careful attention to each of them in turn.

The first factor is simply down to the way the judge perceives you as a person. Before you even open your mouth he will have already made some kind of appraisal of what kind of person he thinks you are. Because of this you should pay careful attention to how you dress for court. There is no strict dress code but you should try and give the image of being reasonable, level-headed and fair-minded. If you have a smart business suit wear that; if not then wear something that looks good on you. Smart casual dress will be accepted better than a tattered old outfit. By all means wear something that expresses your personality but be warned that some judges may have rather different views to yours, so don't dress in a way that might lead to a misinterpretation of your character.

Even more important than the way you look is what you say and how you say it. Always speak clearly, purposefully and in a matter of fact way. Don't talk too fast, don't get emotional if you can help it and above all remain polite and courteous even when directly addressing the opposition. You must sound sure of what you say otherwise you will never appear credible in the eyes of the judge. If you are unaccustomed to speaking in public then practise what you have to say aloud at home before the trial. Split your reasoned arguments into a series of numbered points that you wish to make. Numbering them in this way means that each point is less likely to be overlooked when the judge looks back over his notes when making his final appraisal of the case.

Be ready to expose and discuss the flaws in the opposition's arguments. If you don't criticise their case no one else will, but you must come across as being reasonable. Try not to criticise out of hand to score cheap points; instead, concentrate on the major issues. Say things like 'I can understand how the other party might have thought this to be so but this is simply not the case'. Such statements should make the judge see that you can understand the other side of the argument; that way he is much more likely to believe in what you are telling him. Indeed occasionally conceding the odd minor point to the opposition without sacrificing the main thrust of your argument will often help convince the judge that you are on the whole a reasonable person and in the right. Certainly an intransigent, uncompromising stance in court will only convince the judge that you are an unreasonable sort of person and that will go very much against you.

Interestingly, academic lawyers and psychologists responsible for helping barristers maximise their success rate in court have carried out various studies of the factors which are relevant in persuading a judge. These factors fall into three groups, those relating to witnesses, those relating to the manner in which the witnesses are questioned and those relating to how the legal arguments are presented. The main conclusions of the research are summarised overleaf.

Key witness factors

1. Overly talkative witnesses are not persuasive.
2. Narrative answers are more persuasive than fragmented ones.
3. Exaggeration weakens a witness's testimony.
4. Angry, antagonistic witnesses are less convincing.
5. Overly dramatic witnesses may come across as phoney.
6. Extreme slowness in responding is not convincing.
7. Too many qualifications of an answer are not convincing.
8. The use of unfamiliar words to make an impression may instead be seen as insincerity.
9. New, original or personal descriptions and analogies are more convincing than old hackneyed ones.

Successful questioning factors

1. Personalise your own witnesses and distance yourself from the opposition witnesses.
2. Use variations in question format.
3. Maintain tight control during cross-examination by restricting opposition witnesses to very short answers.
4. Convey a sense of organisation in your presentation of evidence.

It is quite easy to see how each of the factors listed relate to the litigant-in-person. When working on your final preparation for trial you should take them into account. Never be tempted to act too clever in the court-room. Be straightforward, honest and talk in simple, easily understood terms. Most of the witness factors really come down to whether you appear to be telling the truth or not. So tell it, all of it.

THE TRIAL

Almost all cases where larger sums of money are involved are designated for trial rather than arbitration. Such cases are normally heard by a circuit judge. The majority of parties involved in such proceedings will be legally represented, usually by a solicitor for pre-trial matters and a barrister for the trial itself. Don't be put off if you find yourself facing legal professionals in court; remember that lawyers get it wrong and are on the losing side about 50 per cent of the time. Do not expect any favours from lawyers acting against you; they are there in court to win the case for their client. You should nonetheless treat them with the politeness and courtesy they deserve.

5. Adapt your style of questioning to suit individual witnesses.
6. Generally remain poker-faced and save reactions for special deliberate use.
7. Rhythm and pace are important; don't bore the judge.
8. Repetition is useful for emphasis but should be used with caution.
9. Avoid interrupting witnesses.

Successful presentation factors

1. Have a clear structure and explain this framework.
2. Give the listener a theme or schema through which they can analyse the arguments.
3. Give brief summaries to enable the listener to keep track (eg, after each witness).
4. Always interpret the evidence; do not leave room for doubt.
5. Refute the opposition's case: it 'inoculates' the audience.
6. Emotive arguments are very effective in the short term but do not have such a long-lasting effect as rational ones.
7. Occasionally advocating a position against one's own interest can be particularly persuading.

In practice a large number of cases are 'settled in court' by mutual agreement reached just before the hearing is due to commence. An 'in-court' settlement varies from an out-of-court agreement in that the terms are presented before the judge who effectively rubber-stamps the agreement. It is hard to understand why such last-minute settlements are commonplace when it would have been cheaper to settle earlier because the legal costs would have been less. Perhaps it is because the barristers do not generally become involved until shortly before the trial and being specialists in handling court cases they have a clearer idea of the outcome than the solicitors. Alternatively it might be that pre-trial nerves make compromise a little easier. Whatever the reason, be prepared to negotiate with the other side but don't sell yourself short.

The trial begins with the parties and their lawyers being ushered into the courtroom. If the hearing is in *open court* the judge will not normally be present when the parties enter although there probably will be one or two clerks in attendance as well as the usher. Each person representing a party will take a seat on the front row of benches facing the judge's bench, the plaintiff's representative on one side, often the left, and the defendant's on the other. If there is a third party then it is quite likely that the defendant or his representative will end up sitting in the middle sandwiched between the plaintiff and third party. If you are in any doubt as to where to sit then ask the usher. Take the time before the judge enters to arrange your papers on the table and make sure you know where everything is.

After a few minutes the judge will be ushered in; you should stand as he enters. He will then beckon to you to sit before getting down to business. If the hearing is in *chambers* the judge will usually be already seated at a large table and the parties will be invited to sit opposite him. Apart from the judge, no one other than the usher is likely to be present.

The judge will begin by acquainting himself with the parties and will quickly read through the particulars of the claim and the defence, if he has not had a chance to do so already. His first task will be to decide who presents their evidence first. Generally this will be the party who bears the greatest *burden of proof*, in other words the side that has the most facts to prove. This will usually be the plaintiff, as illustrated in Figure 3.5, but if there is a large counterclaim the defendant might begin. Whichever party presents their evidence first will also have the last word at the end of the trial.

The party who presents its evidence first opens the trial with a short speech introducing the subject matter of the case. The presentation of evidence then commences with the calling of the first witness. Witnesses in a full trial always have to swear an oath to tell the truth; while swearing on the Bible is the norm, the Koran and other alternatives are available if needed. The first witness should always be someone who can give a good overall picture of how the dispute between the two parties arose. A litigant-in-person will normally be expected to take the witness stand first before calling any other witnesses and whether you are the plaintiff or the defendant you should always present yourself as your first witness. This will enable you to put across a comprehensive perspective of your point of view. It will also help you quickly get over any nervousness about being cross-examined before your other witnesses give evidence.

The first stage of a witness giving evidence after being sworn in is called *examination-in-chief* and during this stage the witness is encouraged to explain events freely in his own words with little guidance from anyone else. *Leading questions*, by which the questioner suggests or limits any answer, are not normally allowed during this stage of giving evidence. The judge will make notes of all of the evidence so when you are giving evidence give him plenty of time to jot down every tiniest detail. Often the judge or a barrister may prompt an explanation in greater detail. A litigant-in-person may refer to notes to prompt himself but

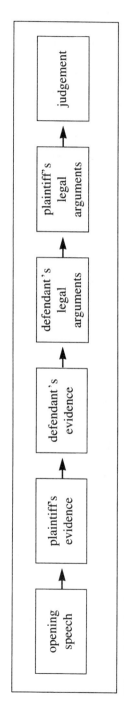

Figure 3.5 *Civil trial process*

remember that when giving evidence one is not allowed to read directly from prepared notes. The formalities of addressing the judge mentioned on p 57 still hold true here of course.

Once the party calling the witness is satisfied that sufficient evidence has been given, the other party has the right to *cross-examine* that witness. This means that the other side may ask probing questions to resolve any contradictions in the evidence or to bring to light what has gone unsaid. Barristers are highly trained at the art of cross-examination and practise special techniques of questioning. Leading questions and those requiring only a yes or no response are permissible during this stage of witness testimony. As a litigant-in-person you may have to both do the questioning and face cross-examination yourself on the evidence you give. Provided that you have prepared properly for cross-examining the other side's witnesses this should not present any major difficulties. Treat the witnesses politely but, should you note uncertainty in their voice, do not hesitate to bring it to the judge's attention by saying 'you don't sound very sure; are you absolutely certain about that' or something similar. It is possible that you may get a very slight rebuke for saying that sort of thing but remember no barrister would think twice about making such a comment. When you are being cross-examined take time to write down the opposition's questions; this will give you more time to think how to answer it. It is perfectly reasonable to ask to be allowed enough time to write down both the questions and your answers for reference later in the trial.

Beware of double-edged questions from the barrister or whoever is cross-examining you; they are easy to side-step if you know how to spot them. Two old favourites are the double-negative question and the multi-question. The former is generally of the form 'Is it not the case that you did not ... a simple yes or no will do' and can be overcome by giving a full explanation instead of the simple yes or no. If pushed for a simple yes or no answer then explain that such an answer to a double-negative question might cause confusion and not do justice to the subject. The multi-question is actually two or three questions rolled into one and is of the form; 'Is it not true that ... and that you ... and so one could say that ...' Again a yes or no answer is sought despite the fact that the answers to the three constituent questions are not all the same. There may even be a double-negative thrown in for good measure. Defeat the multi-question by writing it down, if necessary ask for it to be repeated, and then answer by saying 'I will answer each of those three questions in turn' and then give individual answers to each of the constituent questions.

If you feel the opposition is pursuing the cross-examination too fiercely then tell the judge that you find the manner of questioning a little intimidating. Remain calm and do not let yourself be rushed into giving a wrong answer. After all there is no way a judge would let you badger a witness the way a barrister might be allowed to.

After cross-examination the party who called the witness is allowed to ask further questions relating directly to any line of questioning followed on cross-examination. This stage is called *re-examination* and allows any lack of clarity in the testimony to be cleared up and for any damage to one's case done during cross-examination possibly to be repaired. The witness then stands down and the party then calls its next witness.

It should be noted that there are certain rules of evidence which are quite strictly adhered to in a full trial. *Hearsay evidence* is any statement by a witness that gives second-hand rather than first-hand information such as: 'I heard Mr Smith say that the engineer thought the equipment was faulty.' Only the engineer could give direct evidence of what he actually thought and no one other than Mr Smith or the engineer could give first-hand evidence on the contents of the conversation. If a third person who was not present during the conversation repeats it, it is hearsay. Hearsay evidence is nowadays allowed by virtue of the Civil Evidence Act 1995 where there is no other, more reliable, evidence available. A notice under the Act as described on pp 43–5, detailing the hearsay, should be sent to the other parties well ahead of the trial to ensure that it will be allowed as evidence. Even where it is allowed hearsay will certainly carry less weight than direct first-hand evidence.

Other rules relate to the use of documentary evidence. The Civil Evidence Act 1968, noted on pp 43–5, makes some provisions for exceptions to the general rule that the contents of documents will only be allowed as evidence where a witness is available to give testimony and be cross-examined as to their authenticity. Thus, in normal circumstances, for the contents of a letter sent from one party to another to be allowed as evidence one of those parties must be available to give evidence of it. The party receiving the letter as well as the party sending it may produce it as documentary evidence. A document such as an engineer's report can only be allowed where the engineer himself is available for cross-examination. There are good reasons for these rules of evidence: it is unfortunately surprisingly commonplace for documents of dubious origin to find their way into courtroom document bundles. If you are faced with a suspect document, or other evidence which you feel should not be allowed, do not hesitate to ask the judge for it to be excluded under the rules of court. Remember though that sometimes, particularly if a document in some way contradicts others written by the same party, it can actually help your case. It is important to make sure that all of the relevant evidence in support of your case is given. You will not be given a second chance to go back and give further evidence once your turn is over.

When all of the evidence to be presented by the first party has been given it is the turn of the other party to present theirs. If there is a third party then the judge will decide in what order the remaining parties present evidence. Exactly the same rules of evidence and procedures apply to all parties.

After all of the evidence of each of the parties has been given it is time for the presentation of the legal arguments in closing speeches. This is done by the parties in reverse order, the party which presented its evidence first has the right to the last word and will be last to give their legal argument. The party who began does also have the right in limited circumstances to call further evidence where the judge gives his consent, known as *leave*. This is limited to circumstances where new, previously unaddressed issues have been raised by the other party's evidence.

The legal arguments fall into two categories: the inference of fact from the evidence and the application of the law to the facts. Inferring facts from the evidence put before the court is usually quite straightforward and sometimes patently obvious. Of course each side is going present to their own biased interpretation, so it is essential when giving your closing speech to go over the evidence and the facts you are inferring from it.

Having dealt with the facts you should then address the points of law. Cite the statutes and case law you researched during your preparatory work; don't hesitate to quote passages *verbatim* if they clearly justify your position. If the other side has already presented their legal arguments then take the opportunity to reply directly to these. Remember that during this stage of the trial it is perfectly acceptable for you to read from pre-prepared notes. You may address the issues of what is morally right and just, but remember that the judge must decide the case on points of law. You must make sure you bring to his attention all of the legal issues which support your side of the case. Failure to do so may affect your right to appeal should the decision go against you.

APPLICATIONS DURING TRIAL

Sometimes it will be necessary for an application to be made during the trial. Generally the procedure for this is relatively informal in the sense that it consists of simply asking the judge to decide on a point of procedure. This will often be required where the rules of discovery have not been properly followed or a very late amendment to pleadings is sought. One side will usually argue that they have been taken by surprise and thus do not have a fair chance to respond to the new information. The criteria on which such applications are decided depends on whether or not in the judge's mind the requirements of a fair trial can be met by allowing or disallowing the item. Often it will be conditionally allowed and will then only be later disallowed if the other side can show that the outcome of the trial has been prejudiced by the application. One option open to the judge is to adjourn the trial to give more time for an answer to be prepared to the late amendment or evidence. Very often, however, the late amendment and late discovered evidence will be seen as a last-minute measure and a desperate one too. Needless to say many such late applications fail to have any real impact on the outcome of proceedings.

THE PRINCIPLE OF MITIGATION

Mitigation is a principle that exists in civil law to protect a defendant from having to pay damages that are either excessive or avoidable. Put in simple terms the question of mitigation is simply the question whether the plaintiff could have or should have done anything to reduce the loss for which they are claiming compensation in court. This is a question that really should have been fully considered before the start of court proceedings and is often raised by solicitors defending cases brought by a self-represented plaintiff. Indeed during the trial the judge may even be asked to consider whether the plaintiff was in some way responsible for the loss arising. Where the loss could have reasonably been avoided or the plaintiff was at least in part responsible for the loss occurring, the damages, if any are awarded at all, will be reduced to reflect this. In the eyes of the law everyone has a duty to mitigate and thus reduce as far as possible any loss they suffer.

An illustration of how this principle is applied would be to consider the following example. A farmer agreed to sell a wholesaler his crop of lettuce for £200, the crop to be picked the next day and collected by the wholesaler at the end of the afternoon. The following day the wholesaler arrived and said that due to a fall in the prices at the market he could only pay £150 for the crop. The farmer refused to let him have the lettuces and shortly afterwards claimed £200 from the wholesaler for breaking their agreement. The wholesaler in turn claimed £25 for the time and petrol wasted trying to collect the vegetables.

If the dispute came to trial neither claim would succeed in full; the farmer could have reduced his loss to £50 by accepting the reduced offer of £150 from the wholesaler, or he could have tried selling the vegetables himself elsewhere. On the other hand the wholesaler could have avoided his loss completely by letting the farmer know earlier that he was no longer prepared to pay the full £200. The farmer should be entitled to £50 damages for the breach of the agreement in respect of the price but probably no more than that.

Obviously the question whether a plaintiff has mitigated a loss will depend on the individual circumstances. Where any possible form of mitigating action relies on facts beyond those referred to in the particulars of claim then these facts must be pleaded and therefore incorporated in the defence. So in a case where the owner of a second-hand car makes a claim of negligence following an accident against another driver, the latter must state in his defence that the cost of the repairs to the car was excessive because it was more than the replacement value of the car prior to the accident. It is up to the defendant to prove to the judge at trial that the plaintiff's loss could have been mitigated. That of course depends on the action that would have been required to mitigate the loss. This action must appear both reasonable and possible in the judge's mind. Where the mitigation would have required the plaintiff to spend money and he had none available then the argument that he could have mitigated the loss is unreasonable.

THE JUDGEMENT

Having heard all of the evidence and all of the legal arguments the judge will now be in a position to decide the facts and the points of law of the case. He may be able to do this immediately or he may require time to think the matter over. In complicated cases the judge may even reserve judgement which means that his final decision will not be given until another day. Where this happens it will be necessary to attend court again for the judgement, which is quite likely to be a written one, to be handed down. In other cases the judgement is unlikely to be in writing. Where a judge does not deliver a written judgement you should take great care to write it down yourself in its entirety as the judge delivers it. Any order the judge makes will be delivered in writing.

The judge will commence by going through the facts of the case as he perceives them. Where a fact has been in issue he will normally say how he has arrived at his conclusion. When he has finished explaining his interpretation of the facts he will then address the questions of law raised in the legal arguments. Again he will usually explain how he reached each resolution of the points of law in issue. Finally he will deal with the rights and remedies of the dispute and will make his order in respect of any claim of one party against the other. Any counterclaim or third party notice will also be decided. If damages have been claimed he will decide how much damages, if any, to award. The amount of damages can be subject to appeal by either party, up or down.

Finally the judge will give the successful party an opportunity to ask for their costs of the legal action which he will normally grant. On rare occasion the costs of the successful party will be refused on the grounds that they were in some measure responsible for the dispute arising or at least not being resolved without coming to court. Only in exceptional cases will costs be awarded in favour of the losing side. However, if there has been a payment into court then the situation is rather more complicated. If the award of damages made by the judge in respect of any claim exceeds the amount paid into court in respect of that claim then the successful party can recover their costs as normal. On the other hand, if the award of damages is less than or equal to the sum paid into court then the party who paid in the money must pay the other party's costs up to the date of the payment into court, but will be awarded his own legal costs for the period from the date of payment up to the end of the trial. The logic behind this arrangement being that the successful party should have settled for the money paid into court and withdrawn their claim at that time.

The unsuccessful party may then ask the judge for a *stay of execution* pending an appeal. This will often be granted if the judge thinks a genuine appeal is likely and this has the effect of suspending the judgement and preventing enforcement until the appeal is either heard or withdrawn. If you are on the losing end of a judgement you dispute then do not hesitate to ask for such a stay before the judge leaves the court.

ASSESSING COSTS

Following the award of costs at the conclusion of the trial the amount of costs will be assessed in one of two ways: either they are assessed by the trial judge as a lump sum; or alternatively they are assessed by a process known as *taxation*. In a small claims arbitration costs are limited to the summons fee, plus no more than £50 for loss of earnings by each party or witness, and £200 for each expert. In more complex cases it is better to have one's costs taxed rather than assessed as a lump sum.

The process of taxation begins with the delivery to the court of a solicitor's *bill* detailing all of the work done on the case by the party entitled to costs. The bill is divided into various sections, the first being a written outline of the subject matter of the case. This is followed by a diary of events which details the complete history of the case. Next comes a summary of the work done analysed in terms of the number of hours spent on particular items to which is added a percentage for 'care and conduct' and an allowance for travelling and waiting time. Lastly there is a section where the costs of the taxation procedure can be inserted. The costs of each of these sections is broken down into the time spent for the item together with any *disbursements* or out-of-pocket expenses. Any claim for costs by a litigant-in-person should be in approximately the same form as a solicitor's bill. A sample bill is included in Appendix 1, on p 150.

After being delivered to the court, a copy of the bill is sent to the party who has been ordered to pay the costs. The payer can choose to pay up or to raise objections to the bill. In the latter case the payer is obliged to send, to both the court and the other party, a list of detailed objections to the bill. The other party may serve a reply to these objections and a special taxation hearing is arranged. At this hearing, usually chaired by a court official known as the *taxing officer*, the bill is scrutinised item by item and any sum deemed to be excessive for any particular item of work is suitably reduced. At the end of the hearing the bill is totalled up and the party entitled to costs has to pay a taxation fee at the court office equivalent to 7.5 per cent of the amount allowed. This fee is then added to the total of the bill and a certificate of costs allowed is sent to the payer, who must then send the whole sum including the taxation fee to the other party. The taxation procedure is subject to the right of appeal in the same way as any interlocutory hearing.

ENFORCING JUDGEMENTS

Once a party has succeeded in obtaining a judgement against another party they are entitled to enforce that judgement by a number of means as long as there is no stay of execution. In practice only a percentage of court orders are settled without the beneficiary of the order having to take some enforcement measure or at least threaten it.

It is possible to summon a party owing money under a court order to attend an *oral examination* where questions may be asked and must be answered on that party's financial status. As well as private individuals, company directors may be summoned; their names and addresses can be obtained from Companies House. The procedure is very simple but does involve a fee. Application forms for this are available from the court office. The examination will take place at the county court covering the area in which the person resides or carries on business. The questions may be asked by the party owed the money or by a district judge on their behalf. A wide range of questions may be asked on the personal or corporate finances of the debtor and can include details of any bank or building society accounts, including balances and account numbers, details of any employment or other income and details of any property owned, houses, flats, cars, furniture, etc. The debtor should also be asked whether he will pay the debt now or be prepared to face enforcement proceedings. Usually the debtor is given two chances to attend an oral examination. If he does not attend the second scheduled examination and has been offered sufficient travelling expenses to cover his journey to court and back then he can face possible imprisonment.

By far the most popular method of enforcing a judgement is to apply for a *warrant of execution* against goods, more commonly known as sending in the bailiffs to seize goods. The goods can then be sold to cover the judgement debt. Again the procedure is simple and involves completing an application form and paying a fee. Remember that you will have to show a copy of the judgement to prove the existence of the debt. The fee, as is the case with other enforcement measures, is added to the total debt under the court order. There are strict rules concerning the powers of the bailiffs and anyone considering a warrant of execution should be aware of these before applying for one. The first rule relates to the right of entry: a bailiff may not force his way into a debtor's home although he can use force, with the court's permission, to enter business premises. Even when a bailiff has gained entry he may not take clothes and bedding or the tools of the debtor's trade other than in very exceptional circumstances. If there are not enough goods to cover the debt plus any removal and auction costs then nothing will be seized. Where this is the case a report saying so will be sent to the party owed the money. A bailiff is entitled to accept payment by instalments and may in some instances where the debtor promises to pay execute an agreement with the debtor whereby the goods will not be seized as long as the debt is paid as agreed.

Note that property belonging to the debtor's spouse or other family members cannot be taken. Sometimes complications will arise where goods are seized and someone other than the debtor claims ownership of them. If you think they are the owned by the debtor you may have to become involved in *interpleader* proceedings to determine the true ownership. Legal costs including solicitor's fees are awarded to the successful party, so do not dispute the ownership of such goods unless you are absolutely sure. The bailiff's warrant remains in force for one year but in practice if the bailiffs find nothing worth seizing on the first or second visit it is unlikely they will try again. If necessary a warrant can be renewed upon its expiry. Bailiffs are supposed to send reports every month on the progress of the warrant but in practice you are not normally going to receive a report unless you chase them up for one. Should you become aware of any change in circumstances of the debtor that may affect the execution of the warrant tell the court immediately.

Another way of enforcing a judgement is to intercept wages or salary due to the debtor from their employer. This is called an *attachment of earnings order* and once again application must be made together with a fee to the county court in the area where the debtor resides. Deductions from a person's wages or salary are generally made by instalments which are often fairly small so as to leave the debtor enough money to support himself and his family. The precise amount of the deductions will be calculated by the district judge on the basis of information supplied by the debtor either by post or at a hearing not unlike the oral examination. Again there is the threat of arrest and imprisonment if the debtor fails to respond to the communications from the court. The court also has the power to punish employers and debtors who do not obey an attachment of earnings order or deliberately give them false information.

Similar to the attachment of earnings order is the *garnishee order* whereby funds belonging to or owed to the debtor can be ordered to be paid into court. This is particularly useful where the debtor is self-employed. The procedure is similar to that for an attachment of earnings order except that the financial status of the debtor is not taken into account. In addition to the court fee and application form, an affidavit sworn on oath testifying to the truth of the facts stated on the application must be filed. The affidavit can be sworn at the court office. The necessary details of the money you seek to intercept can be gained from an oral examination; you will need full details of the account name, number and branch details, etc and it would also be wise to ascertain when there is any money coming into the account such as the date on which a salary is paid each month. Time any application to arrive at a time when there is most likely to be some money in the account, and don't forget to allow a few days for the court to send out the necessary paperwork. Once the paperwork is received by the bank or other institution they have eight days to pay the requested sum, or alternatively the balance of the account, into court. Note, however, that the bank or building society is allowed to charge their customer an administrative fee for doing this and that fee is deducted from the account first before the garnishee order is satisfied, whether in part or in full. If for some reason no money is paid into court then a hearing will be arranged before the district judge who can order full or part payment of the judgement debt. But beware, however, that if no money is paid into court because the bank holds no funds belonging to the debtor then it is possible that you will have to pay the bank's and the debtor's legal fees for attending the district judge's hearing; if this is the case then write to the court at the first opportunity withdrawing the garnishee proceedings and send copies of the letter to the bank and to the debtor. It should be noted that a slightly different procedure is required for a garnishee order in respect of funds held by the National Savings Bank which technically is Crown property and thus requires a different protocol; the court office will be able to advise of the proper procedure in this instance.

Where there is a large judgement debt outstanding there are two other means of enforcement available. A *legal charge* can be put on the debtor's property (land or securities) preventing them from being sold without the debt being cleared. Like the garnishee order a completed application form together with the appropriate fee and a sworn affidavit are required. In extreme cases the party owed the money can ask for an order forcing the debtor to sell his home but in reality such orders are rarely granted.

The other option is to commence bankruptcy or insolvency proceedings against the debtor which can be done where the total debt is more than £750. Often, if the debtor has the means to pay but is simply being as awkward as possible about actually paying, the mere threat of such proceedings is sufficient to obtain payment. This is particularly true of large companies who are notoriously difficult to bring to book. The initial costs of serving a bankruptcy petition are very high so this option can only seriously be considered in a limited number of cases. Anyone seriously contemplating bankruptcy or insolvency proceedings against another party should first consult a specialist text on the subject.

None of these means of enforcement can guarantee payment of the judgement debt. For example, if the debt is owed by a company in financial trouble and on the verge of liquidation it will be almost impossible to recover any money at all. The same would probably be true for a private individual receiving income support. Furthermore some small sole traders, partnerships and even limited companies, when pursued for a debt will suddenly vanish without a trace. So be warned and be wary; it is quite possible to win your case and find that all of the time and money you have spent fighting it has been in vain. This is something that should really be considered before starting proceedings.

CIVIL ACTIONS IN THE HIGH COURT

Procedures for civil proceedings in the High Court are essentially very similar to those in the county court only somewhat more exacting. Indeed the County Court Rules and the Rules of the Supreme Court (ie, the High Court) are to be unified over the coming years. Precise details of High Court procedures, and those of the Court of Appeal are given in the *Supreme Court Practice* rule book which can be found in many larger libraries.

There are monetary limits which determine whether a money claim should be brought by means of a *writ* in the High Court or a summons in a county court. At the time of writing all damages claims for less than £25,000 must be brought in a county court and all claims in excess of £50,000 in the High Court. Between these two limits the party bringing the claim can decide in which of the courts to commence their action. Any claim brought in the wrong court will be transferred to the correct court. Any litigant-in-person faced with this choice should think long and hard about which court to commence proceedings in, as there are advantages and disadvantages to both. Proceedings in the High Court attract greater awards in respect of costs so there is more at stake, more to win but also more to lose. On the other hand, the generally slower pace of the county courts gives the litigant-in-person much more time for all that crucial reading. It has to be a personal choice.

Actions that are started by writ in the High Court are served with an acknowledgement of service to be returned by the defendant. The writ must include a *statement of claim* which outlines the cause of action. A *statement of the defence* must be filed within 14 days of the expiration of the deadline for the return of the acknowledgement of service. Summary judgement is available where this is not returned and may also be sought on application where there appears to be no arguable defence. Time extensions of 14 or 28 days may be sought for serving the defence; in the first instance any such request should be addressed to the plaintiff and only if they do not agree does one need to apply formally to the court. Following the service of the defence, the procedure is essentially the same as that in the county court. Claims within the county court financial limits may be transferred there upon the application of either party.

Certain actions such as those for libel and slander (time limit three years from the date of knowledge of the defamation) can only be brought in the High Court, where, unlike other civil matters, they may be decided by jury. The High Court also has jurisdiction to hear *judicial review* proceedings which relate to the powers exercised by public bodies including government departments, local councils, the magistrates' courts, tribunals and even the Legal Aid Board. The Queen's Bench Division is the section of the High Court which normally deals with such matters and has the power to make orders by which these public bodies must abide. These may be orders quashing previously made decisions of a body which has acted beyond its jurisdiction, or where an error of law has been apparent in its procedure. These are known as *certiorari* orders. Other orders called *prohibition* orders similarly prevent any excessive or abusive jurisdiction by a public body in the future. *Mandamus* orders compel the performance of a public duty owed to a private party who has applied to the court for a review of the matter. The type of order sought does not have to be specified in advance by the applicant and damages may also be ordered. The criteria for the granting of any of these orders is that there has been 'procedural impropriety', illegality or irrationality apparent in the exercise of public function. This may result from a failure to act in a proper consultative manner, dishonest conduct or plain lack of reason. There is a three-month time limit for starting proceedings which may relate to education matters, immigration, the rights of homeless persons, mental health patients and prisoners, tax, social security and so forth.

Judicial review is a two-stage process. The first stage is to obtain leave for a review from a judge on the Crown Office List. This is done by filing a notice of application for leave at the Crown Office at the Royal Courts of Justice containing a statement giving the grounds for the application. This must be accompanied by a sworn affidavit verifying the relevant facts. The decision whether or not to proceed with the review may be made on paper (which greatly reduces costs), or alternatively, the judge may choose an oral hearing for this purpose. The respondent may challenge the application for leave. If leave is granted then the matter will proceed to a proper substantive hearing in the Divisional Court. Discovery of evidence is available on interlocutory application and special leave must be obtained to allow the cross-examination of the respondent or for the presentation of any new evidence.

4

Criminal proceedings

The precise manner in which criminal proceedings begin depends upon the seriousness of the alleged crime. In the case of minor offences and private prosecutions, proceedings are begun with the issue of a summons following a complaint by the police, local authority, or sometimes by a private party. This summons will require the person named in it to attend court on a particular date to answer this complaint. Where a more serious crime is alleged then a suspect will have been arrested and charged, and has the right to go before a magistrate ahead of any proceedings proper to ask for bail. In both cases the accused person will have to appear before a magistrates' court where he or she will be tried for the offence or face committal for trial by jury in the Crown Court.

If only a *summary offence* is alleged then it will be tried by the magistrates and in such cases the complaint must be made, or the police information laid, before the court within six months of the alleged offence. More serious *indictable* offences are not subject to any time limit and are usually tried in the Crown Court. In instances where an offence is *triable in either way* the prosecution or the defence may ask for one kind of trial in preference to the other.

There are a number of factors which should be taken into account when deciding which to opt for: these include the size of any penalty (which tends to be lower in the magistrates' court); the time taken to come to trial (weeks in the magistrates' court as opposed to months in the Crown Court); the question of costs (a person found guilty in the magistrates' court will normally be faced with less costs than in the Crown Court while someone who is acquitted is more likely to get his legal costs paid in the Crown Court than in the magistrates' court) and the effect of having a jury (depending on your circumstances, a jury can be significantly more or less sympathetic than magistrates and more driven by emotion). It is also worth remembering that legal aid is much easier to obtain for Crown Court proceedings.

RIGHTS UPON ARREST

Very often criminal proceedings begin with the arrest of a suspect by the police, whose powers to stop, search, question, arrest and detain suspects are governed by the provisions of the Police and Criminal Evidence Act 1984 (PACE for short) and other statutory regulations. In accordance with these statutes the police are obliged to follow guidelines set out in five Codes of Practice issued by the Secretary for State and officers who do not follow the Codes are liable to disciplinary proceedings. These Codes of Practice, together with the new Code of Practice for investigations by the police, the Crown Prosecution Service and other investigators, should be available at all police stations for consultation by police officers, detainees and members of the public. They can also be found in *Stone's Justices' Manual* which is stocked by many public libraries. Evidence relating to criminal proceedings which is obtained by the police in contravention of the Codes may be inadmissible in court as long as the breach of the Codes can be proved.

The first of the Codes of Practice, Code A, deals with the powers of stop and search. The police have the right to stop and search anyone only in the circumstances set out in the Code. The search may extend to the person's car and any bags or parcels they may have with them. In public the search is otherwise limited to the removal of the outer coat, jacket and gloves. A more rigorous search must be out of sight of the public and be carried out by a police officer of the same sex as the person being searched. Intimate body searches must be authorised by a superintendent.

Code B covers the powers of the police to enter and search buildings and the seizing of property. While they have no automatic right to enter and search without a warrant, there are a number of circumstances where this can be avoided. Reasonable force may be used to effect entry and to make any search of a building. A record should be made of any search which must include a list of items seized and any damage that has occurred during the search. Note, however, that the courts have a certain amount of leeway to allow the presentation of evidence obtained from searches where the guidelines have not been strictly followed.

The detention, treatment and questioning of suspects is dealt with in Code C. Arrest is defined as the deprivation of a person's liberty to go where he pleases. Reasonable force may be used to effect an arrest and the suspect must always be told that he is under arrest and why. Restraint may not be used arbitrarily. The police automatically have a full right of search upon the arrest of a suspect. An arrested person should be taken to a police station as soon as possible after the arrest unless his presence elsewhere is necessary for the police to carry out investigations.

Ten things to remember about defending a criminal charge

It can be difficult when defending a criminal charge, and protesting your innocence, to think in terms of getting yourself off the hook on a technicality. Here are a few things worth remembering.

The Police and Criminal Evidence Act Codes
The investigation of criminal offences and the gathering of evidence by the police are subject to strict codes of practice. Evidence, particularly that relating to the interviewing and identification of suspects, may be disallowed at trial if it appears that the codes were contravened. Copies of the codes are available for inspection at any police station.

Alibis
If you have an alibi, it must be disclosed before the trial in order to give the police a chance to look into it. You must provide details of any witnesses who may be able to substantiate it. If you fail to disclose an alibi you may be prevented from calling evidence to support it at trial.

Your plea
Even if you have pleaded guilty by post you can change your plea at trial but you must give the clerk of court warning of this. Unless you are pleading guilty to a very minor offence you must attend court to give your plea in person (or send a solicitor in your absence).

No case to answer
After the prosecution has presented its evidence, and without presenting a defence, you can submit to the court that there is no real case to answer. This can be done where the prosecution case is generally weak or where the prosecution has failed to establish an important element of its case against you. This can be particularly important during committal for trial to the Crown Court.

Has a real offence been committed
Sometimes there will be a question as to whether any real offence has been committed. Have your actions been misinterpreted? Were

you just acting in self-defence? Or perhaps were you taking something to the lost property office without knowing it was stolen? One can always find an alternative explanation of the facts.

Identification evidence
Identification witnesses may only effect an identification in court if they have previously picked you out of an identity parade. Where there is only one identification witness you may wish to question the acuity of their eyesight and their powers of memory.

'Beyond reasonable doubt'
For you to be found guilty, the prosecution must prove its case *beyond reasonable doubt*. This means that you only have to call into reasonable doubt the weakest link in the chain of facts asserted against you to succeed with your defence. You should therefore focus on any lack of certainty or clarity in the prosecution evidence.

Summing up
At the end of the trial you have the right to the last words which should remain fresh in the minds of the magistrates or jury while they arrive at their verdict. Be selective in what you say, and if you have several points to make, number each of them. Don't go on too long.

Mitigating circumstances
If you have pleaded, or are found, guilty, you have the right to make a mitigating speech and call a character witness before sentence is passed. Again this should be kept short and should highlight extenuating circumstances, previous good character and so forth. Prior to sentence you also may ask for other similar or lesser offences to be taken into consideration; this has the advantage of wiping the slate clean of these other offences even though the sentence handed down can still be no more than the maximum for the offence with which you were charged.

Appeals
You have the right of appeal against any conviction and any sentence. Except in cases where new evidence proving your innocence comes to light, there are strict deadlines inside which your appeal must be lodged.

Theoretically a suspect can be detained only if arrested and charged with an offence or if his detention is necessary to gather, secure or preserve evidence relating to the offence for which he was arrested. Anyone who attends a police station voluntarily has the right to leave at will at any time unless placed under arrest. One can always refuse to help the police with their enquiries; there is only a social obligation to co-operate with them. Note, however, that it is a punishable offence to give them false information or waste their time.

On detention a person must be given a written note of his rights, including his rights to see a solicitor in private, to have someone told of his detention and to inspect the Codes of Practice. These rights may be delayed in more serious cases for a number of reasons, for example to prevent the possibility of evidence being destroyed, of co-suspects being warned or the recovery of stolen property hindered. Access to a duty solicitor must be allowed; this can be done under the Green Form Scheme for free without a means test or financial contribution. The general physical conditions of detention are also prescribed by the Code of Practice and make provisions for the rest, sleep and refreshment of detainees.

The detention of a suspect must be reviewed after six hours by the police station's custody officer who is supposed to keep a custody record for every person detained. Further reviews should follow every nine hours after that and at each review the suspect or his solicitor may make representations to the review officer. Normally the suspect cannot be held without written charges for more than 24 hours although in serious cases an officer above the rank of superintendent can authorise further periods of 36 hours up to a total of 96 hours. A magistrates' court can also authorise further periods of 36 hours and the detained person or his solicitor have the right to address the court when the police seek such a prolongation of detention.

Where the police hold a suspect too long without legal right, a writ of *habeas corpus* may be made to the Divisional Court of the High Court; if you are in detention yourself you will need a solicitor to do this for you. Access to a solicitor must be permitted by the police within 36 hours of any request for such a consultation. Where charges have been brought by the police the detained person must come before the magistrates' court at the next sitting on that day or the following day, or the day after that if it is a bank holiday.

A caution must be given when a person is questioned for evidence that may be put before a court. A similar caution must be given after each and every break in questioning. The police have the right to ask questions prior to taking a suspect to the police station, but any evidence which has been obtained in such a way to circumvent the Codes of Practice may be excluded in court by virtue of section 78 of PACE. Bear in mind that while you have the right to remain silent during questioning, silence or evasive responses may later be interpreted by the court as an indication of guilt.

Formal interviews may only take place at a police station. Prior to any interview the detainee must be reminded of his right to free legal advice. He is entitled to have a solicitor present at any time he is being questioned and also has the right to know what the police intend to do if he refuses to answer the questions being asked. A record, usually a tape recording, must be made of the contents of any interview (in accordance with Code of Practice E). The person held in police custody must be allowed at least eight hours continuous rest in any 24-hour period, free from questioning, travel or other interruption.

Code of Practice D relates to identification procedures such as identity parades and the use of photographs. A suspect has the right to insist on a parade taking place and is always entitled to have a solicitor present if he so wishes. Before any parade he should be given a leaflet explaining his rights. The witness making the identification should not be allowed to see the suspect prior to the parade. The persons forming the parade must consist of at least eight persons of similar age height, general appearance and position in life. Two similar suspects may appear in a parade of 12 or more persons. The suspect may select his own position. This position can be changed between each inspection by a different witness. The witness must be told that the suspect may or may not be in the line. The witness may ask to hear the voice of any person in the parade but must be told that the participants were selected for their appearance and not their voice. A suspect has the right to have his comments upon the identity parade noted by the officer in charge.

Identification by photograph should not take place where a parade is possible. A selection of at least 12 photographs of similar style must be shown where this procedure does take place and the witnesses told that the suspect's photograph may or may not be among them. After a positive identification by photograph, an identity parade must be held for all the witnesses. Note that a witness cannot be asked if they see a person in the courtroom whom they connect with the committing of an offence unless they have previously selected that person from an identity parade.

IF YOU ARE ARRESTED

If you are arrested and a simple rendition of the truth is obviously insufficient to obtain your release then I would suggest you consider the following course of action:

1. Refuse to say anything outside of a formal interview. There have been a large number of instances where verbal statements made at other times are put in evidence by the police and denied by the defendant in court.

2. Always insist on your right to see a solicitor even if the police try and dissuade you from doing so. Never answer any questions until a solicitor has been consulted. Even if you later intend to represent yourself at any court hearing it is important to establish a link with someone who can act on your behalf outside the police station and who can also possibly act as a witness in the event of any failure by the police to follow the Codes of Practice.

3. Insist on reading the entire Codes of Practice and insist that they are followed to the letter. If at all possible keep your own record of everything that takes place during your detention, including a record of the contents of all conversations with the police officers involved.

4. It is best to say absolutely nothing immediately after you are arrested because you are likely to be quite upset. Furthermore the statement may give away details of any legitimate defence you have and allow the police to alter their account of what happened.

5. Never say anything without a solicitor or other independent person present. It is always best that there is someone else who can corroborate the contents of any statement you make. If you decide to say something then it is advisable to prepare your own written statement because otherwise arguments may later occur about its accuracy in reflecting what you had intended to say.

6. Never agree to co-operate with the police on the basis of a promise of quicker release on bail or similar. This ploy is not legal because the right to be considered for bail remains even in the face of a suspect's total refusal to co-operate.

7. You do have the right to remain silent although under section 34 of the Criminal Justice and Public Order Act 1994 this silence may be taken to infer guilt unless there is good reason for it, for example if the suspect is very emotional, or confused about the charge. Similar inferences can be drawn from a person's refusal to answer any question unless again there is good apparent reason for the refusal. Note that a suspect can be cautioned at any time, before or after being charged, that if they fail to mention any fact when questioned by the police, it may harm their defence if they intend to rely on that fact in court.

8. If you are guilty then you should have nothing to lose from remaining silent, or, if you find it easier, by answering 'no comment' to each question you are asked. The Law Society currently has guide-

lines that solicitors should advise any client who privately admits his guilt to remain silent.

9. While your permission is not required for the taking of fingerprints, breath samples, photographs and 'non-intimate' body samples such as hair and fingernails, consent is usually required for the taking of 'intimate' samples such as blood, pubic hair, etc. However the requirement of consent can be waived by the police in certain circumstances and any refusal to give body samples can be taken by a court to infer guilt.

10. Never do a deal with the police unless a solicitor or other independent person has been consulted and informed of the deal. This is important because if there is later any uncertainty over the terms of a deal you have someone to back you up.

PROCEEDINGS IN THE MAGISTRATES' COURT

After the issue of a summons or the arrest and charging of a suspect, the summary trial or committal hearing is held in the local magistrates' court. Most magistrates' courts have a duty-solicitor scheme in operation for the benefit of anyone who turns up at court needing legal advice or representation. If there is no duty solicitor present you may be able to get an adjournment to allow you to obtain legal advice elsewhere. On arrival at the court you should report to one of the ushers or other member of staff who will tell you where to wait to be called for trial.

Except in cases triable only by summary proceedings, the prosecution is obliged to disclose to the defence, before the case is heard, an outline of their case against the accused and provide copies of the statements made by their principal witnesses. This duty of disclosure extends to include evidence which they hold and do not intend to present before the court. If this evidence is not supplied early enough to allow reasonable time to prepare a defence, then an adjournment can be sought. As much notice as possible should be given to all concerned of any application to adjourn.

If accused you must attend court on the day of the trial unless you have pleaded guilty by post, which one may do for petty offences only, or send a lawyer on your behalf to deliver the guilty plea. Any accused person who has not done either of the above and does not appear at the court on the day of the trial will be found guilty in his absence or, if the offence carries a possible prison sentence, the magistrates will issue a warrant for his arrest. However, they will only take these measures if they are sure that the summons was properly served in the first place, and instead may insist that the summons is re-issued and served properly. Once charges have been brought by the police, the matter can pass into the hands of the Crown Prosecution Service (CPS), who take over the conduct of the prosecution. The police or CPS may conduct the prosecution themselves in the magistrates' court or instruct a barrister to represent them in the Crown Court.

Figure 4.1 shows the overall course a criminal prosecution may take; but the precise form of proceedings in the magistrates' court depends on the category of the alleged offence with which the defendant is accused. *Summary offences*, the least serious category, are always tried immediately by the magistrates; while *indictable offences*, serious matters such as murder, manslaughter, rape, robbery with violence and burglary, can only be tried by jury in the Crown Court after committal by the magistrates. Certain offences such as theft and common assault are *triable either way* and in such cases the accused is brought before the magistrates where both the prosecution and defence are given an opportunity to state whether they want a summary trial or an indictment. For a defendant, this choice really comes down to deciding between a full and thorough trial in front of a jury in the Crown Court where the chance of acquittal might be slightly better, or a quicker but briefer hearing of the case in the magistrates' court where sentences are often lighter. After hearing the preferences the magistrates will decide which procedure they believe to be most appropriate and act accordingly. A defendant does, however, have the right to insist on a jury trial in the Crown Court although one may be penalised there by way of a stiffer sentence if found guilty.

SUMMARY PROCEEDINGS

The proceedings begin with the defendant, the accused person, being asked to stand while the magistrates' clerk reads out the charges. Where the defendant has been arrested and charged by the police, the police charge sheet will have been handed to the clerk and this becomes the *information* on which the proceedings are based. If the accused has not been arrested the police will have produced written information for the court. It is this information on which the magistrates will generally rely to decide whether to try the case or commit it for trial to the Crown Court, and from which the charges will be read. Following this reading of the charges, the defendant must then reply with a plea of guilty or not guilty. There are two main reasons why anyone might consider entering a plea of guilty: the hope of a lighter sentence and the prospect of avoiding having to pay the further costs of the prosecution.

Following a guilty plea the prosecutor, a police officer or CPS repre-

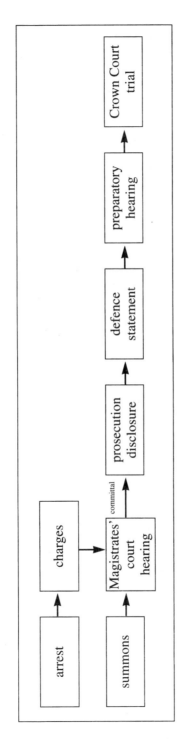

Figure 4.1 *Criminal proceedings process*

sentative, summarises the circumstances of the offence and gives details of any previous convictions, known as *antecedents*. The guilty person is then invited to speak in mitigation to present any facts that might persuade the magistrates to order a lighter punishment. This mitigating speech should always be short and to the point, focusing on either the extenuating circumstances of the crime, or on aspects of positive character in private life such as previous good conduct, family commitments and the honesty shown by admitting guilt. When pleading guilty by post it is possible to present such mitigating factors in a letter enclosed with the guilty plea or on the form itself. The magistrates will consider these facts when pronouncing sentence. Under section 48 of the Criminal Justice and Public Order Act 1994, there is now a statutory obligation for the court to impose a reduction in sentence where a guilty plea is entered. Note that it is possible to plead not guilty in court after having pleaded guilty by post, but if you change your mind like this you must give the clerk of the court advance warning.

If a not guilty plea is entered then the case proceeds to trial or committal. The prosecution will commence with a brief outline of the case and then the first witness will be called. The magistrates' clerk will keep notes of the charges and of the evidence given by the witnesses. The procedure in a criminal trial is essentially similar to that in civil proceedings described on pp 60–66, with each witness first giving their own version of events during the *examination-in-chief* and then the other side allowed to *cross-examine* them. The Criminal Justice Act 1982 took away the right of any witness to make a statement without first swearing an oath. This can technically hinder your ability as a litigant-in-person to argue the facts in the way a lawyer is permitted to, and because of this one should think twice about representing oneself in criminal proceedings.

Leading questions, which suggest or limit any possible answer are normally forbidden in the initial examination-in-chief stage, but are permitted during the cross-examination of any witness by the opposing side. However, if any witness is reluctant or reticent to give evidence, the judge or magistrate may be asked if the witness can be treated as hostile in which case a more forceful line of questioning, including leading questions, may be adopted. After the cross-examination of each witness the prosecution is allowed to re-examine the witness but only to clarify any new evidence raised in the cross-examination.

Having heard all of the prosecution witnesses and after the production of any other evidence, the defence is entitled to submit to the bench that there is no real case to answer. This can be done either where the prosecution has failed to produce evidence to establish some essential ingredient of the offence, or where the evidence produced is so weak, or so discredited by cross-examination, that no reasonable person could reach a guilty verdict.

If the magistrates agree they will dismiss the charge. Otherwise they will decide to continue either with the trial or with committal to the Crown Court. This decision depends largely on the gravity of the offence but also takes into account whether the prosecution or the defence has expressed a preference for either option.

If the case continues to trial you can now give your version of events in your defence and call your own witnesses. Witness orders can be obtained to compel witnesses to attend the hearing; these will have to be arranged in advance of any hearing. The prosecution is, of course, allowed to cross-examine each of the defence witnesses, including you on your evidence, and again this can be followed by the *re-examination* of each witness.

Once all of your evidence has been put before the court the summing up begins. The prosecution always does this before the defence; you always have the right to have the last word with a summary of your side of the case. The magistrates will then pass judgement with a verdict of guilty or not guilty on each of the charges brought. This decision may be made immediately or, if the facts are more complex, the magistrates may retire to discuss the case in private.

Once they have reached a verdict you must stand while it is delivered by the chairman of the bench. If found not guilty then you should immediately ask for the payment of your legal costs. If on the other hand you are found guilty then the prosecution will normally ask for its costs to be paid by you together with a compensation order for the victims of the crime. They will also put before the court details of your past record and antecedents. At this point you are allowed to make a mitigation speech and provide character witnesses who might be able to persuade the bench of the appropriateness of a lenient sentence. It is best to keep this brief; one respectable character witness should suffice. At this point too, it is customary to ask for other offences to be 'taken into consideration', an arrangement whereby these other similar, or lesser, offences go uncharged in return for being taken into account when the sentence is decided. The advantage of this is that you cannot in the future be charged with these other offences if it is agreed now to take them into consideration.

Sometimes sentencing will be delayed for a week or so while a social inquiry report is obtained. This enables the sentencing magistrates to take your home and employment background into account when the sentence is determined. Occasionally sentencing will be deferred for up to six months to give a defendant a chance to prove himself worthy of a light penalty.

Anyone who has pleaded guilty to a more serious offence may be committed to the Crown Court for sentence. Both the verdict and the sentence delivered by the magistrates can be appealed to the Crown Court unless the appeal is only on a specific point of law in which case it can be heard by the Queen's Bench Division of the High Court. It is worth noting that any apparent bias in the behaviour of the magistrates' clerk can give sufficient grounds for an appeal.

COMMITTAL PROCEEDINGS

Where a committal is sought for trial in the Crown Court the procedures may vary from case to case. The traditional 'old style' procedure resembles the magistrates trial up to the point where the defence may ask for the magistrates to consider whether there is any basis of a case against the accused. The prosecution witnesses are called in person, they give evidence and are cross-examined and transcripts of what is said are prepared and signed by each witness. In this form of committal you are under no obligation to disclose at committal how you intend to defend the trial proper. This procedure is long and arduous and hence it is now seldom used. However, if identification is at issue you may be able to insist on this form of committal to the Crown Court. The witnesses cannot be asked if they see in court the person who committed a crime, unless they have attended an identity parade beforehand and picked you out.

Instead of the traditional procedure most committals are made on the basis of documentary evidence including written statements taken from the prosecution witnesses. The prosecution must disclose its case and provide copies of these documents ahead of the hearing for a 'committal on the documents'. (Note that these disclosed documents are confidential and you can be fined heavily for breaching this confidentiality. Only once documents have been given as evidence in open court proceedings does this confidentiality cease.) Often the defence agrees with committal to the Crown Court and the hearing is a mere formality. This is called a section 6 committal as it follows a procedure laid down by section 6(2) of the Magistrates' Courts Act 1980. If there is no agreement the committal proceeds accordingly with the witness statements and other documentary evidence being presented before the court. After the evidence has been presented you can ask for the case to be dismissed on the basis that there is not really any case to answer. The magistrates will then decide whether to commit the case to the Crown Court for trial, dismiss it or proceed with a summary trial themselves. Very complex cases or those involving children can be transferred to the Crown Court without a committal proper. Once you have been committed for trial to the Crown

Court legal aid is normally available both for the bail application and for the trial proceedings. If bail has not already been granted, you can now make an application although normally the question of bail should have been addressed earlier at a separate hearing.

Following the committal you may be required under the Criminal Procedure and Investigations Act 1996 to deliver a *defence statement* which sets out the general terms of your defence and the reasons why you take issue with the facts asserted by the prosecution. Details of any *alibi*, including the identity of witnesses who can support it, must be included, and a failure to provide the defence statement within the standard 14-day time limit can be mentioned at the trial for the jury to make whatever inferences seem appropriate.

On receipt of a defence statement, the prosecution are obliged to review the evidence they hold and make further disclosures of any material relating to issues raised in it. The prosecution does, however, have the right to withhold evidence where it is in the public interest, for example to preserve evidence or prevent vital information falling into the hands of other suspects who have yet to be arrested. Such withholding of evidence and any other apparent non-disclosure can be challenged by making an application to the court to review the situation.

TRIAL IN THE CROWN COURT

There are a number of reasons why you might think twice about representing yourself in a Crown Court trial. Obviously it would be impossible for anyone not granted bail to be able to go out and find witnesses for the defence but even if one does have that opportunity direct contact with the witnesses can be difficult and can also be misinterpreted as to its intent. Indeed it is an offence under section 51 of the Criminal Justice and Public Order Act 1994 to intimidate anyone assisting in the investigation of a crime. Even simply trying to get in touch with a witness might, to that person, appear intimidating. On the whole members of the public are never keen to become involved as a witness in a court case and someone who is upset about the legal proceedings themselves is probably the least suitable person to approach them. (A reluctant witness can be compelled to attend court by serving a witness summons as described on pp 42–3.) It is also very difficult for you to see the proceedings from an impartial viewpoint and it is quite possible that you might concentrate too much on proving your innocence instead of easily getting yourself acquitted on a point of law or other technicality. Legal aid is available for nearly all Crown Court defendants (subject to financial status) and the successful party is usually awarded their costs so legal representation is not normally too great a problem. Working with a lawyer you will probably do no worse than handling the case on your own.

A few months' delay can be expected after the committal proceedings before a case comes up for trial in the Crown Court. Unlike civil cases where the trial is arranged well in advance, the parties to criminal hearings usually get only very short notice of the hearing date. If the case is complex there may be a preparatory hearing ahead of the trial at which the judge will attempt to identify, simplify and narrow the issues in dispute between the two sides. He can order the provision of further details of the prosecution and defence statements, or order evidence to be prepared in a special format for ease of understanding by the jury. Orders made at preparatory hearings as well as those relating to the disclosure of prosecution evidence can be appealed to the Court of Appeal.

The Crown Court trial begins with the *indictment* against the accused being read out. The indictment may contain further charges that were not brought at the time of committal but which rely on basically the same witness evidence. A plea must then be entered of guilty or not guilty on each charge (or *count* as they are called in this context). If there is more than one defendant each may ask to be tried separately; sometimes the judge will allow this but more often than not such a request will be refused.

Following a guilty plea the judge will proceed to pronounce sentence; otherwise, for a not guilty plea, he will deal with any preliminary matters such as ruling on the admissibility of certain items of evidence. If you wish to challenge the right of the prosecution to bring any evidence which may have been unfairly obtained you should do so at this point. Following this the jury composed of members of the public will be sworn in. It is they who will hear all of the evidence and decide the final verdict on each count. The defence has the right to object to potential jurors, up to three without giving any reason and only for stated reasons beyond that number. The prosecution also has the right, on certain grounds, to object to the presence of a witness. Normally a jury must have at least 12 members and once the composition of the jury has been decided and the jurors sworn in the case begins. The overall procedure from this point on is very similar to that in the magistrates' court although here the case will be dealt with in much finer detail following the procedure shown in Figure 4.2.

The prosecution opens the case by giving a brief description of the alleged crime before calling the first witness. Each witness will be sworn in and once they have given their evidence they can be cross-examined by the defence and then re-examined by the prosecution. Great emphasis is placed on the rules of evidence in a full criminal trial and, unlike civil

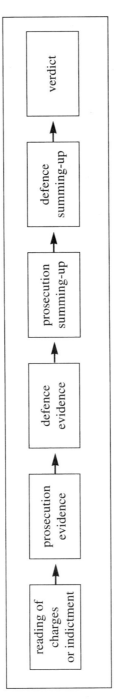

Figure 4.2 *Criminal trial process*

proceedings, there are strict rules governing how the evidence has been obtained. Above all it must have been obtained lawfully within the statutory guidelines laid down in the legislation such as the Police and Criminal Evidence Act 1984. If there has been any undercover investigations or entrapment then the court must consider whether the police in some way enticed the committing of an offence. Also in question will be the evidence for any true offence having been committed and how actively the police were involved, whether there is a corroborated record of what took place and whether information was obtained unfairly when it should have been obtained in accordance with the PACE Codes of Conduct.

All of these criteria have an important bearing on the admissibility of any prosecution evidence. The defence evidence is only presented when all of the prosecution evidence has been put before the court and again it may be submitted that the prosecution has failed to establish an important element of its case or that the evidence is too weak or circumstantial. If the judge agrees he will direct the jury that as a matter of law there should be an acquittal.

Before calling any witnesses, or presenting any other evidence, you are entitled to an opening speech putting the case for the defence in context. Such an opening speech is not allowed, however, where only character witnesses are being presented and/or, as defendant yourself, you only are giving evidence relating to the facts of the case. The evidence is then presented and any witnesses called (including you) may be cross-examined by the prosecution.

Once all of the defence evidence has been heard, the prosecution then starts the closing speeches, followed by the defence, with a final summing up for the benefit of the jury being made by the judge. This closing speech is used not only to review the evidence which has just been heard, but is also used to clarify the inferences that may be drawn from the evidence and to introduce any relevant points of law. The judge will use his summing up to direct the jurors on these points of evidence and points of law, reminding them that for a verdict of guilty the prosecution must have proved its case *beyond reasonable doubt*. Judges are obliged to remind jurors of the difficulties relating to identification evidence and should review all of the evidence, noting any weaknesses in it, during the summing up at the end of the trial before the jury retire to consider their verdict. A failure by the judge to give a full impartial summing up would constitute sufficient grounds for a retrial.

It is entirely up to the jury to reach its own verdict, normally they will be given at least two hours to come to an unanimous agreement. If unanimity is not reached after that time then the judge will direct the jurors to try to reach a decision agreed by a majority of at least ten. A verdict of not guilty may be delivered by a jury but with a verdict of guilty in respect of a lesser offence instead. If after further deliberation no such majority verdict can be reached, this is called a *hung jury*, and the judge may order a new trial to take place in front of a new jury.

When the jury has reached a verdict all parties will be ushered back into the courtroom to hear it formally delivered by the jury foreman. If there is an acquittal then the case is over; the prosecution has no right of appeal against the jury's verdict. You may ask for your legal costs which will in most cases be awarded, but normally no other compensation will be available despite the disruption the court case will have caused to your life.

If the verdict is guilty then the judge will ask for details of your past record. You will then be allowed to plead any mitigating circumstances and to ask for a lenient sentence in the same way as in the magistrates' court (see p 87). These submissions will be considered carefully by the judge together with any social worker's report on your background. Sentence will then be passed and the judge will also consider the situation regarding the costs of the prosecution which will normally be ordered to be paid by the guilty party. A defendant may also be ordered to pay compensation to the victims of the crime of which he has been found guilty.

You have the right of appeal to the Court of Appeal against the verdict and the sentence on any point of law. The prosecution may also appeal against the sentence if they feel it is too lenient. There is also the prospect of a re-trial where an acquittal is 'tainted' by the possibility of intimidation of witnesses or jurors. A relatively high percentage of criminal appeals are successful: in 1995 33 per cent of appeals against conviction and a staggering 69 per cent of those against sentence were allowed (compared to 25 per cent overall in civil cases). Any appeal must be made quickly as strict time limits apply; normally the appeal has to be filed within 21 days after the Crown Court hearing. However, someone found guilty in a criminal case does have the right to seek a review by the Criminal Cases Review Commission at a later date should new facts proving his innocence come to light.

- Decide plea of *guilty* or *not guilty* (previous plea can be changed)
- Decide preference for *summary trial* or *committal* (if appropriate)
- Check prosecution disclosure
- Disclose alibi, make *defence statement* as required
- Prepare argument that there is no case to answer (if appropriate)
- Check that PACE Codes adhered to
- Prepare notes on the evidence
- Prepare notes for questioning the witnesses
- Prepare arguments on questions of fact and law (see also Figure 3.4, p 54)
- Prepare mitigation speech
- Prepare list of other offences to be taken into consideration
- Inform witnesses of hearing, obtain witness summons, etc

Figure 4.3 *Defence checklist*

PROVING YOUR CASE

While in theory the process of the trial itself is largely the same for both civil and criminal cases, in practice there tends to be a great difference in emphasis between the two. In the civil trial there is very often a large concurrence of the facts relied on by the opposing sides and it is the legal interpretation of these facts which is at the heart of any argument. In criminal cases, however, it is much more likely to be the facts which are in dispute and therefore it is the evidence by which the facts can be proved or disproved which becomes the focus of attention. As it is the prosecution who must prove its case beyond reasonable doubt to obtain a conviction, only the weakest link in the chain of facts asserted by them has to be broken for a defence to succeed.

For the requirement of proof beyond reasonable doubt to be met a number of different types of fact must be established and each of these particular categories of fact gives rise to a number of possible defences. The first type of fact that must be proved is that an offence actually took place. The basis of the charges brought by the police may not be the only interpretation of what actually took place. It only has to be established that there is room for reasonable doubt in this respect for there to be an acquittal. There are various types of case that give rise to the option of this line of defence; among these are all alleged crimes where there is no witness other than a sole alleged victim. Such cases usually involve one person's word against another with no other real evidence and are invariably difficult for the prosecution to prove. Very often the outcome may turn on how the witness and accused are perceived and especially on who comes across as the most convincing. The witness factors listed on p 60 are equally important here. Remember though that if a case has already reached court it will generally take more than just an alternative explanation of the facts to convince the magistrates or a jury.

Beyond this category of cases there are several others where the committal of an offence may also be in doubt. In the domain of high-technology fraud in particular, it can be almost impossible to specify and detail what, if any, crime has taken place as computerised money operations are notoriously hard to unravel. Sometimes the question of whether a crime has occurred will be the subject of intense legal argument. Political prosecutions against protesters and peace campaigners often fail to prove that any real offence has been committed.

Another important type of defence relates to the identification of the defendant as the person who has committed the offence. Again the criteria for acquittal is whether it can be shown that there is reasonable doubt that it was the accused and not someone else who carried out the crime. Alibis or other evidence to the effect that the accused person could not have committed a crime are always important in this respect but attention may also focus on general weaknesses in the identification evidence presented by the prosecution. As already mentioned in this chapter, there are strict rules relating to the use of identification and alibi evidence in the court and evidence may be disallowed if correct procedures have not been followed.

Beyond this there are also a number of general defences which may be successful provided the particular circumstances can be proven, at least on the balance of probabilities. These include insanity and diminished responsibility, although these two lines of defence present obvious credibility problems for any litigant-in-person. A state of intoxication may be a defence where the drink or drugs were taken involuntarily or as part of a prescribed medical treatment. Proof of duress or of coercion may also be successful, as can be the necessity of public or private defence. However in cases of self-defence, the defence of others, or the defence of property, the force used must be seen as being reasonable and necessary.

The failure by the police or the prosecution to follow certain procedures before and during trial may also give rise to a number of technical defences. The provisions of the Police and Criminal Evidence Act Codes of Conduct are of particular importance here. Other technicalities in the rules of court may give rise to further lines of defence. For example, a summons that has been issued while the accused person was outside the United Kingdom is invalid and therefore any judgement on it delivered in his absence must be set aside. (Note, however, that this would not necessarily be a bar to any subsequent similar summons being properly granted.)

It is often very difficult for a litigant-in-person to come to terms with the idea that they should search for a technicality to secure their acquittal when they know they are innocent anyway. Once accused there is an overriding desire to clear one's name and prove one's integrity rather than relying on an easy get out. Do not fall into this naive trap: the magistrate, the judge and the jury can all get it wrong. Miscarriages of justice are unfortunately common. Remember that although in theory you are innocent until proven guilty, in practice once you have been charged with an offence you are no longer seen to be innocent until you are found not guilty.

As a defendant who pleads innocence you must do everything in your power to defeat the prosecution. Leave no stone unturned and no angle uncovered by contesting every single fact and every interpretation and inference drawn from each fact. It is your right as a defendant to deny everything and disprove everything that you can that has been said against you. Question whether any offence has been committed, deny any tenuous links identifying you with a crime and argue that evidence has been improperly obtained. If you do not raise these issues no one else will raise them for you. It is hard enough to fight a criminal case on your own but it is even harder to fight an appeal after you have been found guilty and possibly are even in prison.

PRESENTING YOUR DEFENCE

In most criminal cases there is unlikely to be the same need for written submission of legal argument as there is in civil proceedings. Only where there is a legal technicality involved does one need to have pre-prepared materials for the court such as photocopies of law reports or law text books. That does not mean of course that you should neglect the preparation of notes on the evidence for your own reference. The best mode of preparing these notes for trial is the same as for civil proceedings in the county court, as described on pp 51–4, but do not forget the additional issues raised earlier in this chapter too. A few very detailed surprise questions for prosecution witnesses are always a good idea as they may uncover weaknesses in their powers of memory, etc. For example, ask what the weather was like on the day of the alleged offence; you will be able to obtain accurate weather reports for that day from old newspapers which are kept at most reference libraries. Detailed questions about the location where the crime was alleged to have taken place may work similarly well with the use of photographs to verify the truth. An identification witness who wears thick glasses can be asked to say how many fingers you are holding up across the courtroom. Be careful to use this sort of tactic very sparingly as over-use will definitely blunt its effectiveness.

The broad guidelines for presenting one's case described on pp 58–60 also largely hold true in criminal trials too, with the notable exception that any tone of compromise should be avoided. Be self-effacing, yes, but do not cede even the slightest point against you. You are protesting your innocence and no compromise is possible. It is equally important not to let your anger and rage get the better of you because a violent outburst in the courtroom may be seen as a predisposition to violent, impulsive or unreasonable behaviour. That would certainly go against you. Remain courteous to the magistrate or judge; they are independent. Your character and thus, one supposes also, the perceived likelihood of you being the sort of person to commit a crime will be judged in part by your manner in front of the court. Be sure to make the right impression; express sympathy for the victims of crime and show that you understand their need to see justice done.

PRIVATE PROSECUTIONS

Although most prosecutions are handled by the Crown Prosecution Service, the police and other official bodies, it is possible to bring a private prosecution in the magistrates' court. As well as criminal offences the magistrates can deal with public nuisance offences and certain family matters (although technically these are civil rather than criminal matters). The procedure is straightforward and is begun by applying for a summons in the court which has jurisdiction for the area where the defendant lives, or carries on business, if the prosecution relates to that business activity. If you are not sure which court that is you should telephone or go to your local magistrates' court who will be able to give you the relevant address and telephone number. You should then go to that court in person to ask for the summons. Applications for summonses are usually heard at the beginning of the morning's business at about 10 am but it is often a good idea to telephone first to find out what time to arrive.

On arrival at the court you should go to the court office and explain that you wish to apply for a summons. The office staff will give you directions to go to a particular courtroom where you should report to the usher on duty at the courtroom door. You will be required to give your name and address and to state the reason for wanting the summons. It is advisable to have read up on the law enough to be able to state the legal basis for the prosecution, for example, by quoting the name and section number of any relevant statute that justifies your case. You should be able to find this information from *Stone's Justices' Manual* which is kept by many public libraries.

Having done this you will then have to wait inside the courtroom for your name to be called. When your turn comes you should approach the front of the courtroom where you will be asked to take the witness stand. You will be asked to give the name and address of the person you wish to prosecute and must show that you have a true basis of a case against them. The magistrate should be addressed courteously as Sir or Madam, or better still 'Your Worship'. Although you will not have to prove your case at this point you may have to produce some evidence to convince the magistrate to issue the summons. This evidence may be your own testimony or that of another witness or it may be in documentary form, whichever is most appropriate to the circumstances.

The magistrate will then approve or reject the application for the summons as he sees fit. The magistrates must be told of any previous summons relating to the complaint; otherwise any new summons may be invalid. Where an application for a summons has been rejected there is nothing to stop a similar later application supported by further more detailed evidence or further submissions on points of law.

When the issue of a summons has been approved an official note should be obtained from the clerk who has been recording details of the summonses granted by the magistrate. This note must then be taken to the court office from where the summons will actually be issued. To avoid any possible confusion it is advisable to check how the summons will be worded before it is prepared. The court staff will then issue the summons and serve it on the defendant, which is normally done by sending it in the post. Be warned that sometimes on receiving a summons the defendant will apply for a second summons known as a *cross-summons*, to be issued against you which will be heard at the same time.

You will be notified of the date of the hearing which you should attend with all of your evidence. It can be useful to have someone with you at the hearing who can help take notes, find documents and lend you some moral support. The procedure will be the same as for a magistrates' court trial which is described on pp 83–8. If the offence which the defendant is alleged to have perpetrated warrants committal to the Crown Court then the Crown Prosecution Service will take over in the role of prosecutor and the private individual who first brought the action must stand down. The Crown Prosecution Service can also take over any private prosecution and, if they choose, drop it without consulting the person who originally brought it.

Anyone contemplating bringing a private prosecution should be aware that there are certain important considerations which should be taken into account. In particular the possibility of other potential remedies should be looked into, including the option of a civil action in the county court, or the High Court, in place of a criminal one. Indeed there are a number of advantages of taking civil rather than criminal proceedings, not least the fact that if one loses one's case there is no danger of being faced with a damages claim for malicious prosecution. Furthermore the civil courts have a wider range of remedies such as damages or injunctions and require a lower standard of proof. Civil cases are decided 'on the balance of probabilities' instead of having to be proved 'beyond reasonable doubt' and therefore it is theoretically easier to succeed with a similar claim in a civil court than in a criminal court. Certainly most lawyers would rarely advise anyone to pursue a private prosecution.

If someone doing something affects you so much that you are considering taking the drastic step of bringing a private prosecution then it is quite possible that you would be entitled to compensatory damages from that person. If so then start civil proceedings in the county court. If not, be persistent with the police or local authority or whoever usually has a responsibility for dealing with your type of complaint: try and get them to prosecute. If in doubt consult your local Citizens Advice Bureau, solicitor, or other source of advice.

5

Divorce and family matters

Most family cases are dealt with either in the magistrates' court or the county court, with the latter generally having jurisdiction over a wider range of matters. The magistrates' court is empowered to deal with a spouse's maintenance orders, exclusion orders against violent husbands and *affiliation* proceedings in respect of the father's maintenance for the children of single mothers. However, since the Child Support Act, most proceedings relating to maintenance for children are now dealt with by the Child Support Agency (CSA), to whom all applications should be made in the first instance.

The procedure in applying for family orders in the magistrates' court is almost identical to that described for private prosecutions on pp 97–9 but in this instance any hearings being classed as 'domestic proceedings' will be held in private. To a great extent there is an overlap between the areas covered by the magistrates' court and the divorce/family section of the county courts so one often has the choice of bringing proceedings in either. However, if the circumstances involve divorce or require action to be taken against a violent or abusive spouse or partner, the proceedings must be taken in the county court. Furthermore, county courts allow for evidence to be given in written form, whereas the magistrates will require oral testimony. Not all county courts have a Family Hearing Centre; you can look in the phone book or *Yellow Pages*, or ring your nearest courthouse to find out your local divorce or family court.

Legal aid is available for many family proceedings so you could also contact your local Citizens Advice Bureau or any legal aid scheme solicitor. Legal aid may be available in respect of contested divorce arrangements regarding money and children. Note, however, that the statutory charge rule applies to legal aid granted for divorce and other matrimonial issues. Under this rule the costs of the legal assistance are recoverable from the proceeds of any settlement made in respect of the family's assets. Thus, although free legal assistance may have been granted in the first instance, it may not turn out to be free in the long term. Fortunately divorce and family procedures have been simplified in recent years to enable the vast majority of those wanting a divorce or other family court order to be able to act for themselves.

DIVORCE

The procedures for obtaining a divorce are much simpler and more straightforward than those for other classes of court action. Proceedings begin with the delivery of a *petition* which must state the reasons for requesting a formal end to the marriage. You cannot bring a petition for divorce until at least one year has passed since the date of the marriage. The only ground which can be used for a divorce is that the marriage has *irretrievably broken down*. There are five recognised ways of proving that a marriage has irretrievably broken down, as follows.

1. The other partner, known as the *respondent*, has committed adultery and you, the petitioner, find it intolerable to carry on living together with them. Note that gay or lesbian acts do not constitute adultery and a one-night stand is viewed as an insufficient reason on its own without the aspect of intolerability. The intolerability need not be caused by the adultery. It could be entirely unrelated.
2. The respondent's behaviour is unreasonable to an extent that the petitioner cannot be expected to tolerate it. The test of what constitutes unreasonable behaviour will vary from marriage to marriage but will certainly include violence, repeated heavy drinking or making excessive demands on a partner.
3. The respondent has deserted the marriage and has wilfully been living apart against the wishes of the petitioner and with no just cause (eg hospitalisation would be a just cause) for more than two years.
4. The couple have been separated for more than two years and both agree to end the marriage.
5. The couple have been living apart for more than five years. The consent of the other partner is not a prerequisite for any divorce sought for this reason.

When determining these criteria the court will ignore a period of less than six months spent living together in attempted reconciliation. This in effect means that the aggrieved partner has a period of up to six months to come to terms with their spouse's behaviour but note that if the reconciliation endures more than six months the grounds for divorce no longer stand.

Ten things to remember about obtaining a divorce

Legal aid is not available for undefended divorce proceedings and because of this it has become normal for anyone seeking a divorce to act for themselves without a lawyer. Here are a few things to bear in mind.

Try to agree terms with your partner
Fighting over your joint assets can prove very expensive. A solicitor's bill for a hard-fought divorce settlement can easily run into the thousands. Even though legal aid can be granted for this part of the divorce it is repayable under the *statutory charge* rule. It is therefore prudent to try reaching a settlement before commencing the divorce proceedings. Conciliation and mediation services are available to help with this.

It does not matter who is to blame
In terms of the settlement it does not really matter who, if anyone, is to blame for the break-up. Only where there has been particularly gross or excessive behaviour by one of the couple will the court overtly take it into account. The award of legal costs of the divorce, quite low unless contested, is nonetheless likely to be influenced.

The criteria for a divorce to be granted
The irretrievable breakdown of a marriage is the sole criterion, this may be proved in practice by:
1. adultery and intolerability;
2. unreasonable behaviour;
3. desertion for more than two years;
4. living apart for more than two years (and with spouse's consent to divorce); and
5. living apart for more than five years (no consent necessary).

Reconciliation attempts
It does not matter if there has been an attempt at reconciliation provided the total time passed trying to live back together is not in excess of six months. Where a longer period has been spent in reconciliation the marriage is deemed as being potentially saveable.

Defending a divorce
Once proceedings have begun there is little point trying to stop the divorce going through; the simple fact that an end has been sought to the marriage more or less proves that it is dead. You are unlikely to succeed in defend-

ing the proceedings which can become very expensive and emotionally exhausting. If you still hope to save your relationship you would do better to behave like an adult than to fight a pointless battle. After all some divorced couples do eventually remarry.

Children
The court will always ensure that the lives of any children affected by the divorce are disrupted as little as possible. It is preferable that they remain in the same accommodation, attend the same school and generally lead the same sort of life as before. The ownership or tenancy of the family home will probably be made over to the parent with charge of the children.

Maintenance
Both parents are expected to contribute towards the living expenses of the children. Maintenance payments from absent parents are now overseen by the Child Support Agency who can be approached independently of any divorce proceedings. A parent who has stayed home to look after the children can also expect maintenance for themselves although this may only be awarded for a limited period.

The one-third rule
As a very general rule the wife will receive about one-third of the couple's joint assets, but this will vary greatly from case to case. Where the woman has been the main bread-winner she will be more likely to receive two-thirds. The one-third rule is really only the starting point from which the apportionment of the family's assets is tailored to their individual circumstances.

The clean break
By being given a clean break, young and childless couples who have not been married long will be put in a position to make a fresh start after the divorce. The court may order joint assets to be sold and the proceeds shared.

The procedure
The divorce petition can be obtained from your local divorce court or county court and is quite easy to fill out. Once completed it should be returned to the court together with the £150 fee. A copy will be sent to your spouse who must acknowledge its receipt and state within 8 days whether they intend to object to any of its contents. Provided that no objections are raised the court will ask you to provide a sworn declaration, called an *affidavit*, on the basis of which they can proceed to pronounce the *decree nisi* without the necessity of a hearing. Where the petition is contested the district judge will convene a hearing, in private, to settle all unresolved matters before making the decree. The *decree absolute* will be pronounced after six weeks provided no further developments arise.

As an alternative to divorce, *judicial separation* may be petitioned for less than a year after the marriage but this remains a relatively rare procedure. Currently some 70 per cent of divorces are awarded on the grounds of unreasonable behaviour and around 25 per cent are awarded on a no-fault basis.

'For richer, for poorer, for better or for worse ...' the traditional marriage vows stand for little in the courtroom. In fact they seem to get the same treatment as unenforceable terms in civil contracts do under the Unfair Contract Terms Act 1977. The criteria of unreasonable behaviour has to be applied individually to each separate case. For example, a wife who refused to let her husband drink or smoke at home, or even watch TV on Sundays was seen as unreasonable; so was the DIY fan who liked to mix cement in the living room. A low sexual appetite on the part of a man is not usually viewed by the courts as being unreasonable whereas on the part of a woman it is!

Anyone wishing to apply for a divorce can obtain the petition form and a number of helpful official booklets from their local county court family section. Much of the form is self-explanatory and simply requires the completion of the names, addresses and occupations of the spouses, details of any children, details of any voluntary maintenance and the grounds for seeking the divorce. Particulars must be provided of the irretrievable breakdown of the marriage and of any unreasonable behaviour or adultery. The particulars should be an outline of the dates and events that have taken place but need not go into any great detail. General guidance on drafting particulars is given on pp 25–7. Finally a section known as the *prayer* needs to be completed giving the names of the children whose custody is sought, the name of the respondent to be served with the petition and the *address for service* which is the address to which the court will send all correspondence. In adultery cases the name and address of the *co respondent* (ie, the person with whom the respondent committed adultery) may (but is not required to) be included, or if it is genuinely not known 'man unknown' or 'woman unknown' should be entered.

If there are any children an eight-page *statement of arrangements for children* form must be completed with details of proposed arrangements for their accommodation, education and financial care, as well the arrangements for the respondent's access to them. The form is very straightforward and also requires details of any special health care needs and of any existing care or supervision orders for the children to be included where applicable. All children under the age of 16 must be included plus any between the ages of 16 and 18 receiving full-time education. A brief description of the proposed place of residence of the children should be given in the residence section, stating clearly whether it is a house or a flat, whether it is owned, rented or council accommodation, the number of rooms and any other details relevant to the children's circumstances, such as a garden or proximity to a sports centre, etc.

Three copies of the forms, or four in an adultery case, must be signed and delivered to the court together with the appropriate fee and a copy of the marriage certificate. Copies of marriage certificates can be obtained from the Registry Office in the district where the wedding took place or alternatively from the General Registry Office in London. For those on very low income it is sometimes possible to be exempted from having to pay the court fee, currently £150, but exceptional circumstances will have to be proved. Persons in receipt of income support or family credit will be exempt from paying the fee.

Once the court has received the petition it will serve notice of the petition on the respondent, as well as the co-respondent if one is named. Included with the notice is a copy of the petition and, if applicable, a copy of the statement of arrangements for children. A special reply form, called an acknowledgement of service, is also included, which the respondent has to return to the court within eight days.

A number of answers are required to questions asked on the acknowledgement of service form including confirmation of receipt of the petition and an outline of the response to it. In particular the respondent must specify whether they intend to defend the case by trying to prevent the divorce going through, defend the claim for costs by denying responsibility for the breakdown of the marriage, or just object to the arrangements for the custody of the children. Additionally the respondent is asked if they wish to apply to the court on their own account for custody of the children or better access to them.

If the case is to be defended, or any of the arrangements opposed, then the respondent must file a formal *answer* to the petition. This answer must be filed with the court within 28 days of receipt of the petition and should address each of the points it raises, including those in the particulars and the prayer. Any points not addressed by the answer will be deemed to have been admitted or agreed. Above all the answer must make it clear exactly what in the petition is opposed and what is accepted. Very often it will only be the blame for the breakdown of the marriage which is in dispute and the respondent may wish to *cross-petition* for divorce, in other words they may seek a divorce themselves on grounds other than those stated by the petitioner. Where this is so, the answer must state the grounds on which the cross-petition is based and give particulars.

In a very small minority of cases the divorce itself will be opposed and once the petition has been served there are only a limited number of defences that can be raised by the respondent. The respondent can deny that the marriage has irretrievably broken down by contesting the truth of the particulars stated in the petition or alternatively, in the case of at least five years' separation, claim that *grave hardship* will be caused by the divorce. Such defences rarely succeed and even then generally only in cases involving older women who might lose the right to inherit the provision of a pension or similar.

Once the acknowledgement of service of the petition has been received by the court the procedure varies depending on whether or not the petition is contested. The various options are shown in Figure 5.1. If the petition is unopposed then the petitioner will be asked by the court to swear an affidavit verifying that the facts stated in the petition and the particulars are true. The affidavit can be sworn at the court office free of charge (or in front of a solicitor for a small fee). The case is then subject to a 'special procedure' where it is put before a district judge who will examine the papers and, provided he is satisfied that the requirements of the divorce law have been met, he will issue a certificate and set a date for a judge to pronounce a *decree nisi*. No further hearing is necessary and if there are no further developments in the six weeks after the decree nisi, a *decree absolute* will be granted and the marriage dissolved. If, however, the district judge finds that the paperwork is insufficient, the court will write requesting further written information or alternatively fix an appointment for the petitioner to come to the courthouse to supply the information in person.

Affidavits may be sworn on the Bible, the Koran and any other holy book or on an affirmation of the truth. However, it might be worth taking your own copy along; once I saw someone have to wait more than an hour while the court staff found a copy of the Koran.

If the divorce is defended or there is a cross-petition then a different procedure will be followed and the case will be listed for trial to be heard in open court by a judge. Witnesses may be called and the trial itself will be similar in procedure to the county court trial described on pp 60–66. Although the hearing may be open to members of the public, there are reporting restrictions relating to all family business in the courts which prevent the publication of any evidence brought in such a case. In any event, the arrangements for the children and any money matters will be dealt with privately 'in chambers'. In reality, however, divorces rarely reach trial.

In contested divorces the real issue is never the question of who is actually to blame for the breakdown of the marriage, instead it is merely a shameless ritual of scoring points to nudge the scales of justice in favour of one party or the other when it comes to finalising the financial

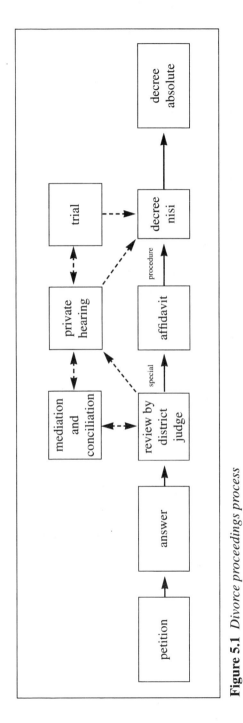

Figure 5.1 *Divorce proceedings process*

arrangements. Of course, human nature being what it is, there may be some bad feeling when a couple part but fighting over every last penny is not going to make anyone feel better. A judge hearing a hard-fought divorce case may easily conclude that both parties are to blame for the break up and accordingly order each spouse to pay their own legal costs. Thus it is very important to reach amicable agreement on financial matters. Avoid this trap and be reasonable; agree terms with your spouse before going to court. If at first they will not be reasonable, try and talk them round; would they really rather see your joint assets wasted on solicitors' bills? Certainly you will both end up losing more in the long term if there are heavy legal bills for a courtroom battle, than you would if the two of you had instead given a little in a spirit of compromise.

- Married for at least one year?
- Marriage irretrievably broken down according to one of the five criteria?
- No more than six months spent attempting reconciliation?
- Attempt mediation or conciliation if divorce is likely to be contested
- Agree financial arrangements (if possible)
- Agree arrangements for children (if possible)
- Complete divorce petition (three copies/four in adultery case)
- Write up particulars of breakdown of marriage
- Complete statement of arrangements for children
- Write up details of any agreed financial arrangements
- Supply copy of marriage certificate
- Supply copies of any previous custody or maintenance orders, etc
- Pay court fee (£150) unless exempted

Figure 5.2 *Divorce checklist*

If you are currently considering seeking a divorce you should be aware that there have been new proposals put before Parliament that may result in broad changes in divorce proceedings. In the future, and it is not known yet when such changes, if any, will be effective, there may no longer be any need to meet one of the five criteria listed above for showing the irretrievable breakdown of a marriage. There could be simply a one-year reflection and consideration period from the date a sworn statement is received by the court made by either spouse stating their belief that the marriage has broken down. During this one-year period all of the arrangements for children and finances will be reached via a process of counselling, mediation and conciliation.

CONCILIATION

Conciliation in respect of divorce proceedings may take place either in or out of court. In court it takes the form of a *pre-trial review* by a district judge in the presence of both partners and the court's welfare officer. Solutions will be sought for the issues that the couple are unable to agree between themselves. The different possibilities for settlement will be discussed and each side will have the opportunity to air their preferences. If no consensus can be reached then the matter will proceed to trial and a judge will decide all outstanding areas of the settlement. This can be very costly for both parties if at this stage they rely on professional legal representation.

Out-of-court conciliation or mediation may also be offered to the couple and may sometimes be achieved in a manner somewhat akin to the arbitration procedure applied to small claims in the county court. A number of recognised bodies exist that can provide this type of service, including the Divorce Conciliation and Advisory Service, the Family and Divorce Centre, National Family Mediation and the Family Mediators Association, all of whose addresses can be found in Appendix 3, on p 160. Conciliation and mediation generally prove much cheaper than employing two solicitors each on an hourly fee to fight over terms. It can be sought prior to initiating divorce proceedings.

FINANCIAL MATTERS

While in divorce proceedings, culpability for the breakdown of a marriage may marginally influence the financial arrangements settled by the court, the overriding concern of the judge will be to ensure that the settlement is both fair and workable. Indeed, nowadays, the behaviour of the spouses is only taken into account where it would be unfair to disregard it. Conduct must be obvious and gross (eg, physical violence, dissipation of family assets or dishonesty) for one side to be deprived of some financial provision. A number of legal principles are applied by the judge to the individual circumstances of the couple to achieve this end. The court will take into account the income, earning capacity, property and other resources of each spouse together with their financial needs, obligations and responsibilities. Also taken into consideration may be such factors as each spouse's standard of living before the breakdown of the marriage, their ages and states of health, the duration of the marriage and the contribution each has made to looking after the home and the family.

One common solution is the *clean break* which is applied to marriages which have been of short duration. If both spouses are young, have always worked and have no children then the courts will probably make no maintenance order. The shared assets may be divided equally or in the ratio of the contributions each has made towards their purchase. Other property will be divided according to who owned it before the marriage. The value of joint pensions and life assurance policies will also be taken into account.

Where children are involved, the situation is different because maintenance will almost invariably be ordered for them. The provision for the children always comes first in any financial arrangements. Not just the children of the marriage itself will be considered but also any other children who were living as part of the family. If they are very young then the spouse who does not have custody of them will probably also be expected to pay some maintenance to the spouse who looks after them. If one spouse has not worked during the marriage, again the court will normally order that the other spouse pays maintenance, although sometimes this maintenance will only be for a limited period.

There are also other solutions available to the court which may involve a lump-sum settlement or an order in respect of the couple's property. Sometimes instead of maintenance the judge will order that one spouse pays the other one large single payment. In other circumstances the court may order that the ownership or the tenancy of the home be signed over to the parent who will keep custody of the children and then award only minimal maintenance payments for them. The right to reside in the family home will nearly always go to the parent who has care of the children. If the ownership or tenancy of the home is not transferred then sometimes it will be ordered that the spouse with custody over the children live there until the youngest child leaves home, at which time the property, if owned, will be sold and the proceeds divided between the couple. Sometimes the immediate sale of the home will be ordered and the proceeds split between the spouses. It is entirely in the discretion of the court to do what it thinks best for the particular circumstances of any family. The judge will of course listen to any suggestions from either partner but his decision is the one that matters. Of course a judge's decision in divorce proceedings can be appealed in the same way as any other civil judgement.

The amount of maintenance awarded will vary greatly from case to case but very often a principle known as the *one-third rule* laid down some years ago in a Court of Appeal case is used as a starting point. Under this principle the wife (usually) can generally be expected to be awarded around one-third of the gross combined family income. In very rough mathematical terms this is approximately the husband's and wife's combined income divided by three, less the wife's own income. But it must be stressed that this calculation is only a starting point and the court will look into what money is left to each of the couple after taking into account mortgage or rent payments, national insurance and pension contributions and so forth.

Anyone faced with the prospect of a forthcoming divorce should seek advice from the Citizens Advice Bureau, a solicitor or other source on maintenance, lump-sum awards and other financial matters. While representation in undefended divorce proceedings is never covered by legal aid, the out-of-court advice may well be free. Any professional advisor should be able to cover the complex tax situation concerning divorce settlements. Any maintenance received is taxable income although the person paying can claim tax relief up to the extent of difference between the single person's allowance and the married person's allowance in respect of maintenance paid under an order of court. A lump-sum settlement on the other hand made out of the family's assets may be free of tax and have the added benefit of making more of a clean break.

It is worth noting that there are sometimes tax advantages for the payer of maintenance to pay under an order of court rather than by informal voluntary agreement. It is therefore always best, even if one can reach agreement on money matters without the court's assistance, to have the arrangement officially recorded by the court. Obviously this has advantages too for the party receiving the maintenance: should the payments not be made as agreed they can be more easily enforced. It should be noted that orders for the maintenance of a spouse normally end when the person receiving the maintenance re-marries or if the person paying it dies. An exception to this general rule may arise when the maintenance payments are secured against property or other assets.

The court has powers to make orders relating to divorce settlements before the divorce itself is finalised. *Orders pending suit* are interim orders made by the district judge immediately upon the filing of the divorce petition. Periodical (ie, monthly or weekly) maintenance payments may be ordered and these can be backed up by being secured against the other spouse's assets. Lump-sum payments are another possibility. Injunctions will sometimes be made to prevent one partner disposing of assets prior to the finalised divorce and the courts also have the power to set aside transactions that have already taken place, although in reality this type of order may be very difficult to enforce.

CHILDREN

The prime concern of the court will be to ensure that suitable arrangements are made for the children of the divorced family. Generally the care of the children will go to the mother, especially if the children are still young. Often the court will try and keep all of the children together if possible rather than splitting them up. Most county courts now have a *welfare officer* who can look into the personal circumstances of the family and make recommendations to the judge. The welfare officer can also call a conciliation hearing between the two spouses where there are disagreements over access to the children. Any children over the age of 11 can also attend such hearings to give their own views.

The court will try and ensure, whatever arrangements are made, that the children's lives are disrupted as little as possible by the divorce. If practical, arrangements will be made for them to stay in the same home, attend the same school and generally lead, as much as is possible, the same life as before. Orders relating to the care of the children of unmarried mothers can be obtained separately in their own right as divorce procedures are obviously inapplicable in such cases. In the county court any family order sought outside of divorce proceedings should be begun by an *originating application*, a procedure outlined on pp 32–4.

Since the passing of the Children Act 1989 court procedures relating to the care of children have been simplified with the courts intervening only where necessary when the parents cannot agree suitable arrangements for their care. Once again the option of conciliation may be offered to the divorcing spouses as an alternative means of arriving at a solution. The welfare of children is now seen as the overriding concern with the old traditional idea of parent's rights ceding to the more modern notion of parental responsibilities for the children. Now even children themselves, or any interested adult, can apply to the court for an order relating to their care, including even matters relating to their adoption. In any arrangements made by the court the wishes of the children must be considered alongside their physical and emotional needs, their background, the likely effects of any changes in their circumstances, any harm the children have suffered or might suffer in the future as well as the capabilities of each parent (or any other person) of meeting the children's needs.

A greater flexibility in granting orders given to the courts under the Children Act allows them to consider what is best for each child. The judge is no longer limited to just approving or rejecting any order which has been specifically applied for and now has the freedom to make whatever order appears most appropriate in the circumstances. New terminology introduced by the Act has largely succeeded in making the resolution of family matters less adversarial and, aside from the emotionally charged atmosphere surrounding such court cases, the proceedings themselves are relatively simple and straightforward. Applications under the Children Act for orders relating to the adoption or welfare of children made outside of divorce or other family proceedings may be made at magistrates' courts, the family sections of the county courts and in the High Court.

Anyone presently seeking maintenance payments for children can make an application to the Child Support Agency, a government agency set up specifically to assess, collect and pay out children's maintenance. The courts now have only limited powers to make maintenance orders for children. The Child Support Agency will deal with most cases. The big advantage of using the Child Support Agency is that the applicant avoids any liability whatsoever for legal costs because the service is free. The Agency can be contacted before the start of divorce proceedings, as soon as the parents have separated or once a parent fails to maintain a child. The telephone number and address of your local Child Support Agency Office appears in the *Yellow Pages* local information section as well as in your local telephone directory. Contact them immediately the maintenance of any child becomes a problem. Note that maintenance payments are equally due from unmarried fathers, but if a father does not admit the paternity of a child then this issue may have to be proved in court.

The assessment made by the Child Support Agency of the level of maintenance required in each individual case takes into account not only the needs of the children but also those of the adults who care for them. Likewise taken into consideration are the incomes and financial requirements of each parent together with any other material circumstances. While there is a standard amount for the weekly care allowance for each child, higher levels of maintenance are payable where the absent parent has a larger assessable income. There was much public criticism of the work of the Agency when it first became operational under the Child Support Act of 1991, but since then the assessment procedures employed have been improved. Certain safeguards have been introduced particularly to avoid unduly penalising parents who have become part of a new family with new obligations.

OTHER FAMILY MATTERS

As well as divorce, maintenance and matters relating to the care and custody of children, the courts have powers to deal with other family problems. These measures often relate as much to unmarried couples as they do to married couples, and include orders relating to the exclusion of a violent or abusive person and orders relating to the disposal of shared property and assets.

In cases of domestic violence the police should always be contacted and the victim should immediately seek temporary refuge with a friend, relative or recognised shelter. The police, local authority social services or Citizens Advice Bureau will be able to help your contact the latter. In cases of child abuse it is probably easier to talk to the NSPCC in the first instance. Never, never make the mistake of thinking that a violent or abusive situation will blow over or somehow work itself out: it will not. Violent and abusive behaviour almost invariably repeats itself.

An *originating application* should be made as soon as possible to the local county court seeking either an *exclusion order* or a *non-molestation order*. If divorce proceedings have already started these orders can be sought on an interlocutory application, a procedure explained on pp 48–9. These orders may be sought *ex parte* without notice being given to the aggressor and will be dealt with very promptly by the court, usually on the day they are received. Such *ex parte* applications will always be allowed where a spouse or family member is so frightened of the aggressor that some protection needs to be afforded against a possible violent response to the court action. An affidavit should be filed with the application which should explain the full circumstances making the order necessary. Legal aid is normally available for such applications when made through a solicitor: use it if you qualify. If, however, you need to act without a solicitor, make the application in the morning when a judge is more likely to be free for immediate consultation.

So called *exclusion orders* affect the violent or abusive spouse or partner's right to enter or occupy the home. Before making any such order the court will consider the conduct of both partners, not just the aggressor, together with their needs, resources and all other relevant matters such as the ages of any children, ownership or tenancy of the home, etc. The possibilities for alternative accommodation for each spouse or partner and the children will also be considered.

Non-molestation orders have a wider scope. They can extend to cover harassment outside the home which cannot be covered by any exclusion order. It is worthy of note that there does not have to be actual violence before these orders can be sought: threats or generally abusive behaviour constitute sufficient grounds for such an order to be granted. An example of a typical non-molestation order application and its supporting affidavit is given in Appendix 1, pp 151–3.

Although some of the details in the affidavit may be embarrassing or painful to include, all of the relevant facts must be stated. Be frank and honest, even about any adultery you may have committed. Never be tempted to exaggerate or lie as this may go against you if the application is contested.

6

Industrial and other tribunals

Outside of the courts system there exist a number of specialised tribunals which, through proceedings akin to the county court small claims arbitration procedure, have jurisdiction over specific fields ranging from employment, immigration and social security right through to property, land and tax matters. From all of these tribunals, many of which are free to use, there is a right of appeal to the courts, although often the case must first pass via special appeals tribunals. The general fashion of preparing and presenting a tribunal case is pretty much the same as that described in Chapter 3. All tribunal proceedings are subject to potential judicial review in the High Court.

THE INDUSTRIAL TRIBUNAL

The most well known of the tribunals is undoubtedly the industrial tribunal which has the power to deal with most aspects of employment law. Notable exceptions, however, are actions in respect of health and safety regulations, injuries at work, and tax or social security matters. The Central Office for the Industrial Tribunals and the Department of Employment issues a series of free booklets which detail all of the matters that can be dealt with by industrial tribunals.

The time limits for bringing a claim at an industrial tribunal are, in most cases, three months from the date the wrong was done, but is sometimes six months. Late claims may be brought in exceptional circumstances. There are a number of official and unofficial organisations which are able to offer specialised advice, support and sometimes even representation in specific categories of cases dealt with by industrial tribunals. Trades unions, women's rights and other action groups are all worth trying alongside the more traditional sources of help.

Ten things to remember about going to an industrial tribunal

The industrial tribunal is a free service provided by the Department of Employment with responsibility over most areas of employment law. Procedures are kept quite simple and informal making it easy for anyone to represent themselves.

Jurisdiction
Unfair dismissal, redundancy, discrimination, sexual harassment, equal pay, maternity leave, trade union membership, written reasons for dismissal and so forth; most aspects of employment rights are dealt with by the tribunal.

Help and advice
Trade unions, law centres and Citizens Advice Bureaux can all provide guidance. Where the problem is of a racial or sexual nature then the Commission for Racial Equality and the Equal Opportunities Commission, respectively, can help and sometimes even provide legal representation.

Time limits
Strict time limits exist for bringing a matter before the tribunal. You have a period of three months (six months for certain types of complaint) in which to apply.

Making an application
To refer any matter to the tribunal you need to complete Form IT1 which is available from Jobcentres, Unemployment Benefit offices and Citizens Advice Bureaux. You will need to give details of yourself, your job, your employer and the circumstances giving rise to your complaint. Make a copy for yourself before you send it off.

The response
Once the completed form is received by the tribunal, a copy will be sent to your employer together with a reply Form (IT3). This reply has to be returned within 14 days if the employer wishes to put their side of the case at the tribunal hearing. The grounds on which they

intend to defend the case must be stated and if these are not clear you have the right to ask for *further and better particulars* of this defence.

Before the hearing
After the delivery of a defence there may be a preliminary hearing to clear up any preliminary matters; otherwise a date will be arranged for the hearing proper. You will need to sort out various documents to bring with you to the hearing, including your contract of employment, staff rule book, pay slips, tax forms and social security papers, etc, as appropriate.

The hearing
The hearing is relatively informal and the precise procedure is decided by the chairman who is usually an experienced lawyer. Each side is entitled to explain fully their side of the dispute and to call witnesses. After having heard both sides the tribunal will retire to consider its decision. This decision may be delivered on the spot or sent out later in the post. Before leaving you can claim travelling and loss of earnings expenses from Department of Employment funds for yourself and for your witnesses.

The decision
The tribunal has the power to award compensation and to order the reinstatement of a person to their job. The amount awarded is calculated according to strict formulae which vary depending on the nature of the complaint. Money awards unpaid after 42 days can be enforced in the same way as a court judgement through the county court and an employer who ignores a tribunal decision can be ordered to pay increased compensation.

No legal fees
No legal costs are *normally* awarded by the industrial tribunal so you will be better off representing yourself than having someone act for you. If hire a solicitor you will have to pay his fee out of your own pocket regardless of whether you win or lose. A 'no-win no-fee' service will have to be paid for out of your award.

Appeals
The tribunal's decision can be appealed to the Employment Appeals Tribunal.

UNFAIR DISMISSAL

An *unfair dismissal* occurs when an employee of more than two years' standing is sacked without good cause. It may be that the underlying reason behind the sacking is unfair, such as personal bad feeling between a manager and one of his staff, or it may be that the way in which the dismissal was handled was unreasonable, for example where proper disciplinary procedures were not followed. Very often both factors are important and when such a case comes before an industrial tribunal it is usually up to the employer to prove that the reasons for the sacking were fair and that proper procedures were followed. The rules concerning unfair dismissal generally cover all employees with some limited exceptions (eg policemen, seamen and crown employees).

A number of grounds are accepted as being reasonable for the termination of a person's employment:

1. a lack of aptitude, or a lack of the necessary qualifications for doing a job, where training has been attempted;
2. misconduct, dishonesty, absenteeism, poor timekeeping or non-cooperation with the employer;
3. genuine redundancy (see p 120);
4. where there is a legal reason for discontinuing someone's employment, such as the lack of a work permit or a driver's disqualification from driving; and
5. some substantial reason such as economic necessity, or ill-health.

Even if the employer can prove that the reasons for a dismissal were justifiable, the dismissal may still be found to be unfair because it was not handled reasonably or did not follow proper procedures. Normally these procedures would be part of the employee's contract of employment but even if there is no such contract it is generally expected that the employer should give as much warning as possible ahead of a potential dismissal situation. This does not, however, apply to cases of gross misconduct, such as assault, other violent behaviour, embezzlement or theft, where no warning is required and on-the-spot dismissal is permissible.

There is sometimes a question of whether or not an employee has actually been dismissed, for example it may not be clear if a drunken worker was sent home for good or just for the rest of that day. No one should ever presume that they have lost their job for good unless they have been specifically told so. In the normal course of events there is not usually any problem because a dismissed employee will be given proper written notice and will have received their P45 tax form. The crucial criteria is that the employer has chosen to dispense with his employee's services and that the employee did not leave of their own volition. Thus the failure to renew a fixed-term contract may constitute dismissal. Refusing a woman her old post after maternity leave certainly does. Note, however, that a person who has resigned may claim *constructive dismissal* in circumstances where the employer has made life so difficult that they were forced to leave, though the employee would need to prove that this was the case.

Any employee who is dismissed and who has worked for his employer for more than two years has the right to know why. Where an employer has failed to give written reasons for a dismissal within 14 days of a written request for such details, the dismissed person may apply to an industrial tribunal to enforce this right and to also seek compensation of two weeks' gross pay for the employer's default.

WRONGFUL DISMISSAL

In certain cases a dismissal may be deemed as being wrongful rather than unfair, perhaps because an employee ultimately wanted to leave a job, but wrong in law, maybe on the grounds that they are cheated out of a period of notice, pay in lieu of notice, accrued holiday pay or bonuses or some other benefit guaranteed by their contract of employment. These conditions of employment include not only the written terms of the employment but also any other conditions which could reasonably be seen to be implied in the contract. Wrongful dismissal is often called breach of contract.

A good example of the distinction between wrongful and unfair dismissal would be where an employee hands in her notice, indicating that she intends to leave her job in six weeks' time to take up another position elsewhere, and is immediately escorted out of the building, told never to return and is not paid any basic pay, commission, bonus and holiday pay that would have been due right up to her intended departure date. The remedy in this situation would be to make a claim to the industrial tribunal for wrongful dismissal to recover the money she should have properly received. The termination of an employment by the employer where the contractual period of notice is not honoured, or pay not given in lieu, is a wrongful dismissal and is similarly actionable. Any action for arrears of pay where there is no unfair dismissal, for example on the expiry of a fixed term temporary contract, can also be addressed to the industrial tribunal. If you have missed the three-month time limit for making your claim at the industrial tribunal, then as an alternative you can make your claim to the county court which can also deal with such matters, and has much more generous time limits.

REDUNDANCY

Redundancy is a special category of dismissal where the employee is entitled to a compensatory redundancy payment. Only employees with more than two years' service are eligible and it must be shown that the employee's work has ended as a result of one of the following circumstances:

1. the business is closing down, either completely or in part;
2. the business is moving and it is unreasonable to expect the employee to move with it; or
3. the need for the type of work that the employee was doing has reduced or gone entirely.

No redundancy payment needs to be made where suitable alternative work is offered and turned down. If an employee is offered a new position they are allowed a number of weeks' trial in that post to check its suitability without losing the right to a redundancy payment.

Employers are supposed to give as much warning as possible to any staff likely to be faced with redundancy and are obliged to consult any recognised trade union involved in the business. In practice, however, it is very much up to the individual to ensure that his or her rights are respected and be willing to enforce those rights through the tribunal.

DISCRIMINATION AND HARASSMENT

Race, sex and disability discrimination in the workplace are dealt with by the industrial tribunals, which includes other practices of discriminating against employees on other grounds including marital status or religion. Discrimination may take the form of biased selection for employment or promotion, or it may be in the guise of unequal treatment. Do bear in mind that there are certain jobs which may reasonably and legally, by their nature, be restricted to a particular category of person. Outside of the workplace, for example in the areas of housing and educational opportunities, discrimination and harassment cases are dealt with in the county court, or by High Court judicial review, both subject to a six-month limitation period.

Harassment can also be a criminal offence and can be reported to the police. Anyone faced with any type of discrimination should at the earliest opportunity contact the Commission for Racial Equality or the Equal Opportunities Commission who will assist in dealing with the problem. At very least you should consult your local Citizens Advice Bureau or other advice centres.

Sexual, racial and disability harassment (which is anything, including comments, and inappropriate topics of conversation, relating to sex, race or disability that is unwelcome by the recipient) are specific forms of discrimination amounting to victimisation, and thus may be dealt with by an industrial tribunal. While other remedies are available, including action in the county court for damages and even criminal sanctions in serious cases, the easiest place to deal with harassment at work is in the industrial tribunal. It is crucial to report any such problems to a superior at the first possible opportunity and to ask them to do something about it. The person causing the harassment must be told, preferably in writing, that such behaviour is unwarranted, unwanted and unacceptable. If the harassment continues then an application to the tribunal can be made on the grounds that it is discriminatory to expect any person to endure more difficult conditions of work (caused by the harassment) than another person of different race or sex doing the same job. In more serious cases one can resign and claim constructive dismissal. In complaints of discrimination, there is no requirement (as there is with many other matters dealt with by industrial tribunals) that you must have worked for the employer for more than two years. Indeed it is possible to bring a claim even if you were *never* employed by than employer at all (eg, if you were turned down for a job because of your race).

AWARDS

The industrial tribunals, as well as being able to award compensation, can order the reinstatement or re-engagement of a person to their old job. The basic award for unfair dismissal and redundancy cases is calculated according to a strict formula which takes into account the length of service of the employee, their age and the value of lost wages. This formula is as follows:

1. a half week's pay for every year of completed service between the ages of 18 and 21; plus
2. one week's pay for every year of completed service between the ages of 22 and 40; plus
3. one and a half weeks' pay for every year of completed service between the ages of 41 and 64 (special rules apply within a year of 65).

Only the most recent 20 years of employment will count; and there is a limit to the amount of a week's pay that is allowed to be claimed which is currently £210. The tribunal can then add on compensation for, for example, loss of earnings up to the date of the hearing (if the employee is still unemployed), loss of earnings in the future after the hearing (though usually no more than three or six months' worth), and (in discrimination cases) injury to feelings. There is an overall limit to the amount tribunals can award of, currently, £11,300, but this limit does not apply to discrimination cases. Note that the employee is under a duty to mitigate his loss (which usually in effect means that he has to go out and find another job as soon as he is dismissed). Mitigation is dealt with more fully on pp 67–8.

Other compensatory awards are available in respect of the other areas of tribunal jurisdiction and awards can also be made where an employer fails to comply with any tribunal ruling.

Additionally industrial tribunal monetary awards can be registered with and enforced through the county court in the same way as a county court judgement (see pp 70–3).

INDUSTRIAL TRIBUNAL PROCEDURE

The application form for taking a matter to an industrial tribunal is Form IT1. This form is also available from most Jobcentres, Unemployment Benefit Offices and Citizens Advice Bureaux. At the same time it is advisable to request any of the leaflets which might be applicable to your case. The form itself is laid out as a questionnaire which is quite simple to complete with all of the details relevant to your application including the grounds of your claim, the identity of your employer and the length of your employment. Outside of the usual time limits an application will normally only be accepted if there is a very good reason for the delay in referring the matter to the tribunal.

The completed IT1 form is sent to the industrial tribunal covering the area where the employer's premises are situated. Once the completed IT1 form is received by the tribunal, it is vetted to see if the subject matter of the application falls within the jurisdiction of the tribunal. The form will be returned to you if it appears that the nature of your claim is not within their scope. Even if your form is returned you do have the right to insist that the application proceed; although be warned that if you do this you may end up having to pay the other side's legal costs if your claim is dismissed. If you have not already obtained expert advice you should certainly consider seeking it if your application is returned. It may be the case that you have grounds for a claim in the County Court instead.

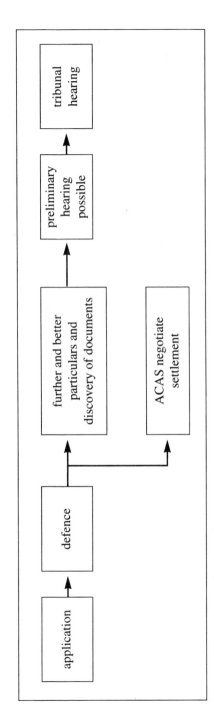

Figure 6.1 *Industrial tribunal process*

Once accepted, a copy of the completed form is sent to the employer (or other party named in the application) who has 14 days to reply by giving their version of events on a separate response form (IT3). On receipt of this completed response form, proceedings follow the course shown in Figure 6.1. A date will eventually be set for the hearing. The Advisory, Conciliation and Arbitration Service (ACAS) may become involved. They will be sent copies of both statements by the tribunal and may, where they see fit, approach each side with a view to arriving at a conciliated settlement. No party is under any obligation to accept any settlement offered at this stage. If agreement is reached this way it should be formalised immediately in writing; ACAS will normally prepare the written settlement for the parties to sign. Once the agreement is signed your case can be withdrawn.

Where the employer's defence is vague or evasive you may request further and better particulars in the same manner as described on pp 37–8. You also have the right to ask your employer for copies of any documents relevant to your case and this should always be done, as it often brings to light helpful matters. Should they refuse to supply these documents you should write to the tribunal explaining why you need them and they will intervene on your behalf.

There may be preliminary hearings where there is any doubt about the grounds of a claim or to deal with other matters. These may be called by the tribunal itself, possibly at the request of one of the parties. Rarely, where a party to proceedings appears to have a very weak case, the tribunal will ask them to lodge a deposit of up to £150 lodged which is forfeited if they lose.

There is a special procedure in *equal pay* claims to ensure that the claim meets certain criteria. This procedure must be completed before any full hearing can be arranged, and consists of establishing whether:

1. the work carried out by employees of each sex is broadly comparable;
2. the work has previously been rated as being equivalent, or
3. the work of any other individual being used as a comparison is really of equal value.

Full hearings are open to the public and it is a good idea, if you have the time, to go and watch one before your hearing is scheduled. The tribunal normally consists of a chairman, often a barrister or solicitor of at least seven years' standing, and two lay members, one drawn from among eligible employers' representatives (eg, the CBI) and the other drawn from among employee representatives (eg, the TUC). Occasionally there will only be one lay member.

Proceedings are similar to the small claims arbitration (see pp 56–60) and the exact procedure is usually decided by the chairman. In unfair dismissal cases it is often the employer who is asked to state his case first, in other cases it may be the employee. Witnesses can be called by either side and their evidence is given on oath (or affirmation) and cross-examination is allowed. Witness orders can be sought to compel reluctant witnesses to attend. Sometimes the chairman will direct that each side state its case before any witnesses are heard; in other instances he may ask for the evidence to be heard in chronological order regardless of who is presenting it.

After all of the evidence has been heard each side is allowed to make closing statements summarizing their arguments. The tribunal will then retire to confer and reach their decision which will usually be read out in the presence of the parties later the same day. A majority decision is required and where there are only two persons sitting on the tribunal the chairman has the deciding vote. Complex decisions may be *reserved*, delivered later and sent out in the post to the parties involved. The reasons for the decision will generally be stated but where they are not either party has the right to ask for full written reasons within 21 days of the hearing or of the date of notification of the decision by post.

Remedies that can be ordered by the tribunal include re-instatement to an old job or cash compensation. The tribunals have the power to order further monetary settlements where their decisions are not complied with within 42 days.

Normally no costs are awarded unless a claim appears to have been brought frivolously or vexatiously or conducted in an unreasonable manner. Allowances towards the travelling and subsistence expenses for you and your witnesses may be met from Department of Employment funds and should be claimed from the clerk of the tribunal immediately after the hearing. A similar provision is applicable for the reimbursement of any lost earnings which result from attending a tribunal.

There is a right of appeal to the Employment Appeals Tribunal and then on to the courts (and also by way of judicial review). An appeal can only be made on a point of law, on a point of fact inferred from evidence (no new evidence is allowed), or on a matter of procedure, and must be sent in writing direct to that tribunal within 42 days of the original decision. The Employment Appeals Tribunal is usually chaired by a judge sitting with an employers' representative and a union representative. Despite the fact that legal costs are not normally awarded it is common for barristers and solicitors to represent large companies at appeal hearings.

Sometimes, in limited circumstances a tribunal will review and amend its own decision when asked to do so in writing within 14 days of reaching a decision. This may be possible where:

1. there has been an error made by the tribunal;
2. an essential witness has been unable to attend;
3. proper notice of the hearing was not received by one of the parties or witnesses;
4. new evidence has come to light which would have influenced the outcome of the hearing; or
5. any other reason dictated by the needs of justice.

SOCIAL SECURITY APPEALS

An appeal to the Social Security Appeals Tribunal must (in most cases) be made within three months of the assessment, review or decision appealed against. The grounds of the appeal must be laid out in writing. A special form (which can be found in leaflet NI246) is provided for this purpose but is not obligatory. If a specific point of law is involved this must be stated. The *Adjudication Officers Guide*, outlining the procedure for the tribunal, is published by the Stationery Office (1997) and can be found in libraries and Citizens Advice Bureaux.

After receipt of your initial written appeal you will be sent a set of *appeal papers* (also known as the *adjudication officer's submission*) that detail the provisions of the Social Security Acts which are deemed by the adjudication officer to be relevant in your case. This is the justification for the decision against which you are appealing that will be presented at the tribunal. Study the appeal papers closely for any errors of fact, omission or interpretation and prepare yourself to explain in detail how the decision is wrong. You should be prepared to provide documentary evidence where necessary; this may be in the form of medical reports, pay slips or even statements from social workers and other witnesses. Copies of the all important 'code books' which cover the whole social security legislation can be consulted at any DSS office.

The tribunal is normally chaired by a solicitor or barrister of at least five years' standing sitting with two lay members, one of whom may be a doctor in cases concerning medical issues. The chairperson should simply be addressed Mr Chairman or Madam Chairwoman. At the hearing the DSS representative (called the *presenting officer*) presents the justification for the DSS's decision first and then you have the right to put your case. The *presenting officer* is often allowed a reply after this. The procedure is, however, flexible and you may be asked to put your case first. Explain your case by giving an outline first followed by the detailed evidence, then fit the evidence to the regulations before finishing with a short summing up. In general an oral decision will be made by the tribunal there

- Check that proper grievance procedure followed
- Check legal basis of claim
- Seek advice/help from trade union, CAB, local authority, Commission for Racial Equality, Equal Opportunities Commission, etc
- Complaint within jurisdiction of industrial tribunal?
- Within time limits?
- Completed two years service? (necessary for some but not all types of case)
- Complete Form IT1 with details of employment and history of complaint
- Prepare notes for reference at the hearing
- Sort out contract of employment, pay slips, etc to take to hearing
- Inform witnesses of hearing, obtain witness order if necessary

Figure 6.2 *5 – Industrial tribunal checklist*

and then, followed by a written decision a week to ten days after the hearing. Before leaving the hearing you should, if necessary, make a claim to the clerk for the reimbursement of any wages lost and travelling expenses incurred attending the tribunal.

Upon receipt of the tribunal decision you may have the right of a further appeal direct to the Social Security Commissioners but you will need, within six weeks, to seek permission from the tribunal chairman first. If this permission is refused then you can within further six weeks make an appeal direct to the Commissioners. Any application for an appeal should be addressed in writing in the first instance to the clerk of the tribunal.

OTHER TRIBUNALS

The procedures for going before the other categories of tribunal are largely similar to those described in this chapter. Almost invariably there is a requirement for each side in a dispute to furnish the other with a written outline of their case before any hearing. Similarly there are provisions for the disclosure of documents and the calling of witnesses. The hearings, though less formal than those in the county court, follow somewhat similar guidelines and the general mode of preparation and presentation of cases discussed in Chapter 3 is certainly applicable.

7

Appeals

There is a right of appeal against most decisions reached by a judge or magistrate delivered in any court proceedings. An appeal is effectively a referral of the case to a higher authority who may ratify, or set aside, any decision reached in the original proceedings. In the normal course of events any appeal will be directed up to the next level of judge within the hierarchy of courts as described in Figures 1.1 and 1.2 on p 2. Appeals may be made on questions of law by way of legal argument, on questions of fact derived from evidence, or on both. In criminal cases both a guilty verdict and the sentence imposed as a result may be appealed against. In civil cases the scope of any appeal is normally limited to only those questions of law and fact which were put before the court at the original hearing. The decision of a judge to allow or disallow specific evidence may itself give rise to grounds for an appeal. So may any procedural irregularity during the original hearing.

Where there is no automatic right of appeal, permission or *leave* of the court must be sought to allow the appeal to be made. Procedural and interlocutory decisions made in a case may, as well as being appealed, also be subject to judicial review in the High Court. Arbitration and small claims decisions can be appealed but normally the leave of the district judge is required for this. Any decision reached with the consent of both parties can never be appealed against. A fee is payable for registering an appeal and the award of the legal costs of the appeal usually follows the outcome. Legal costs in the Court of Appeal can be very high. At present a backlog of cases is waiting to be heard.

Hearings are very straightforward and generally similar to those for court proceedings in the county court. Debate is generally restricted to the specific points cited in the *notice of appeal* and does not facilitate a total review of the whole case. Only in the Crown Court does an appeal amount to a total rehearing of a case.

There are strictly-adhered-to time limits for filing any appeal; so do not delay if you think you should proceed with one. Where no new evidence is allowed, reliance is placed on the judge's notes of the hearing or on a transcript of the original trial, if one exists, which is seldom. Note that the judge's interpretation of the evidence put before the court can constitute a question of law. If you find yourself on the receiving end of a judgement that is clearly wrong then you should ask the judge for a written *judge's note* (or *statement of case* in criminal proceedings; see below) explaining how he reached his decision. You can ask for very specific questions of law and fact to be addressed in this way. A request for a judge's note can be made verbally to the judge at the hearing. A written request can be made afterwards to the courthouse office but this should be done promptly.

APPEALS IN THE COUNTY COURT

An appeal to a judge in the county court against a decision made by a district judge must be made within 14 days of that decision. All interlocutory decisions in the county court are subject to appeal, in the first instance to a circuit judge at county court level and then subsequently in the Court of Appeal. Appeals may also be made to the county court from an external source such as a rent assessment committee or local council planning department, and must normally be made within 21 days of the decision being appealed against (or the time limit specified on the written decision of that body; if different). In all cases a *notice of appeal* must be delivered to the court accompanied by a copy of the judgement, order, decision or award appealed against. A copy of the judge's note should also be submitted where one has been given. The grounds for the appeal should be put as politely as possible in the circumstances; eg: 'The Honourable District Judge erred in his inference of fact from the evidence and misdirected himself in the application of legal argument to ...' The space for the date should be left blank for the court office to complete once a hearing has been listed. A sample notice of appeal is given in Appendix 1 on p 154.

The party making the appeal, the *appellant*, must provide a copy of each of these documents for the court and a further copy for service on the *respondent* and any other party affected by the proceedings. The notice of appeal must clearly state the grounds upon which the appeal is made. A hearing in front of a judge will be scheduled at which first the appellant and then the respondent are entitled to argue the specific points of law or of fact. New evidence may be allowed with the consent of the judge where it was not possible or reasonable to produce that evidence for the original process (eg, in planning applications). Many county court appeal decisions can be further appealed in the Court of Appeal.

- Within time limits?
- Identify the court in which to appeal, apply for leave if necessary
- Apply for a *judge's note* or *statement of case*
- Decide the basis of your appeal
- Review the evidence
- Prepare arguments on the inference of fact from the evidence
- Review the legal arguments
- Prepare further or more detailed legal arguments
- Review the original trial procedure
- Prepare legal arguments on points of procedure (if appropriate)
- Appraise sentence (or the amount of damages in civil case)
- Prepare arguments against sentence (or amount of damages)
- Complete *notice of appeal*
- Write up *skeleton arguments* for submission to court
- Prepare photocopies of law books, law reports, etc for the hearing
- Pay court fee (civil appeals only; currently £80 County Court, £20 Court of Appeal)

Figure 7.1 *Appeal checklist*

THE COURT OF APPEAL CIVIL PROCEDURE

Civil appeals to the Court of Appeal from the High Court or the county court must be filed within 28 days of the decision, order or award being appealed against. There is an automatic right of appeal to the Court of Appeal for all final judgements in matters involving more than £5000; in cases where a lesser sum is at stake leave to appeal must be sought in writing either from the original court or from the Court of Appeal. Again multiple copies of the notice of appeal, the decision appealed against and any other relevant documents must be served, in this instance at the Appeals Office at the Royal Courts of Justice. A further copy must be also served on the original court or tribunal where the decision appealed against was made. The notice of appeal must state the category of appeal under which the appeal is to be listed. List categories include:

- County courts: final and new trial list;
- County courts: interlocutory list;
- County courts: divorce, final and new trial list;
- County courts: divorce, interlocutory list;

and so on with equivalent lists for the High Court, tribunals and other sources. The Court of Appeal office will be able to advise you of the appropriate list category; alternatively a full list can be found in the *Supreme Court Practice* rule book which gives the prescribed format for the notice of appeal, full procedural details as well as the complete rules of court for appeals.

On receipt of the notice of an appeal the respondent has the opportunity to reply to the notice and may, if so desired, also enter a separate appeal of their own, called a *cross-appeal*, against the relevant judge's decision. The grounds on which any cross-appeal is based must be stated in the respondent's notice. Alternatively the respondent can contend that the Court of Appeal should uphold the decision which the appellant is challenging. Once again there is a strict time limit for delivering the respondent's reply to the notice of appeal.

Sometime after the respondent's reply is received by the Appeals Office the appeal will be listed for hearing and the appellant is then required to lodge a bundle of relevant documents with the court. This bundle must include copies of the appeal notice, the respondent's reply, any official transcript or record of the original hearing or trial where the decision appealed against was made, and any evidence put before that hearing that relates to the appeal.

Once a date has been set for a hearing of the appeal, the parties involved will be notified and any party wishing to heard at this hearing is required to serve, on the Court of Appeal as well as on the other parties involved, a document outlining the *skeleton arguments* of the case they intend to put before the court. These skeleton arguments must be served within 14 days of the case being listed for hearing. Note the cases which need to be dealt with rapidly are assigned to a special waiting list called the *short-warned list*. Hearings for cases on this list are called on short notice and in this case the court office will give a specific date by which the skeleton arguments must be served.

The appeal hearing is not a retrial of the case but is limited to only the issues raised in the notice of appeal/cross-appeal and to arguments already disclosed in skeleton arguments. Except in exceptional circumstances no new evidence is allowed and much reliance is placed on the transcript or judge's notes from the original trial. Legal argument is normally intense and often quite a lengthy judgement will be given stating the full reasons for the final decision.

In the Court of Appeal any party who is faced with the prospect of an appeal by the opposition may avoid the costs of the appeal hearing by answering the notice of appeal with a statement that they agree with the judge's decision being appealed against and intend to take no part in the hearing other than as a spectator. Beyond cases covered by this provision the costs of the appeal are normally awarded to the successful party. Precise details of Court of Appeal procedures are available from the Royal Courts of Justice Court of Appeal office and can also be found in the *Supreme Court Practice*. There is a Citizens Advice Bureau in the Royal Courts of Justice building which also can help in case of difficulty.

APPEALS FROM THE MAGISTRATES' COURT

From a decision made in the magistrates' court appeals may be made either to the High Court or the Crown Court depending on the type of case involved. The Crown Court will hear appeals relating to a conviction or sentence from a criminal offence, a binding over, contempt of court order or any decision relating to liquor, betting and gaming licences. Other matters such as adoption and family proceedings, questions of law and jurisdiction, or any application for *certiorari*, *mandamus* or *prohibition* orders will be dealt with on appeal by the Divisional Court of the High Court. These orders may be used to vary, quash or prevent any sentence delivered in the magistrates' court and are equally applicable to those handed down in the Crown Court. The procedure for obtaining such orders is dealt with on pp 73–5.

Appeals from the magistrates' court must be served within 21 days of the decision which is being appealed against; where a sentence was delivered later than the date of conviction this time limit is calculated from the date of sentencing. The precise format for each of the different forms of appeal can be found in Part 9 of *Stone's Justices' Manual*. Any party who intends to appeal on a point of law to the High Court should ask the magistrates' court to *state a case* for the opinion of the High Court. The application to state a case must be in writing and must clearly identify the questions of law or jurisdiction which the High Court will be asked to decide. The powers of the magistrates' court are subject to judicial review by the High Court, a practice explained on pp 74–5. The costs of such an application can even be awarded to be paid by the magistrates themselves where they have acted beyond their remit.

CROWN COURT APPEALS PROCEDURE

Appeals heard in the Crown Court against judgements delivered in the magistrates' court may be made in relation to questions of law or fact. The appeal can take the form of a rehearing of the whole case and new evidence that was not brought before the magistrates is allowable. The Crown Court has the right to award any punishment that would have been available to the magistrates even if it is more severe than the original sentence. Anyone who originally pleaded guilty may only appeal against their sentence while a defendant who pleaded not guilty may appeal against both the conviction and the sentence.

For Crown Court appeals no special form of notice is prescribed and there is no requirement to state the exact grounds of the appeal; for example, a general statement that 'the conviction was made against the weight of the evidence' or 'the sentence is excessive in the circumstances' will suffice. The notice of appeal must be served on the Magistrates' Court within 21 days of the decision being appealed against. The notice must clearly state whether the appeal is against conviction, sentence or both. Two copies should be given to the Clerk of the Court and one to the prosecution. A sample notice of appeal from the magistrates' court to the Crown Court is given in Appendix 1, on p 155. The Crown Court does have a wide discretion to allow an extension of time for an appeal to be made where there is good reason to do so, as would be the case where fresh evidence comes to light which needs considering. Bail and legal aid may be granted for Crown Court appeals.

HIGH COURT *CASE STATED* APPEAL PROCEDURE

You must first make an application to the magistrates' court or Crown Court to have the case against you formally 'stated' in writing. This application must be in writing and be delivered within 21 days of the decision being appealed against.

The magistrates' or Crown Court will then consider the application. The particular magistrates or judge who made the original decision may refuse to state a case on the grounds that the application is frivolous; otherwise they will issue a statement of the case. Where the stating of a case is refused you still have the right to seek a *mandamus* order from the High Court, by way of the judicial review procedure, to compel the original court to state their case. Similar provisions for stating a case relate to tribunals and other official bodies.

Within ten days of receiving the stated case, you must draft a written case for the appeal and file it together with the stated case at the Crown Office department of the Central Office of the Supreme Court at the Royal Courts of Justice. Copies must also be served on the other parties involved in the case within four days of lodging the case at the Crown Office. A notice of the entry of the appeal must be served on the CPS or other respondent.

COURT OF APPEAL CRIMINAL DIVISION

Applications may be made to the Criminal Division of the Court of Appeal to entertain criminal appeals from the Crown Court. Appeals against conviction may be on the grounds that no reasonable jury could have reached such a verdict, or may be made by way of legal argument against conviction or sentence, and may only be brought with leave of court. Only in very exceptional circumstances will any new evidence be admitted. This is mostly likely to be so where new evidence comes to light that was not available at the time of the original trial and which might acquit a convicted person. Even when the normal appeal deadline has passed such cases can be referred to the Court of Appeal by the Criminal Cases Review Commission (CCRC). Cases which have originally been appealed to the High Court may also be referred to the Court of Appeal via the CCRC. Requests for leave to appeal to the Court of Appeal, or for consideration by the CCRC, must be made in writing. The addresses are at Appendix 3, on pp 160–6.

Only very rarely are criminal appeals heard by the House of Lords, which is technically the final court of appeal, and even then question appealed is usually restricted to points of law of great public importance.

8

Scottish law

The legal system in Scotland varies in a number of respects from that found in England and Wales. Scottish law is distinct from English law having developed independently over the centuries. Serious criminal matters are dealt with by *indictment* and are heard in the senior courts by a judge and jury, while less serious offences are subject to the *summary complaint* procedure without a jury in the lower courts.

The High Court of the Justiciary is the most senior criminal court in Scotland and hears all appeals as well as having exclusive jurisdiction in the first instance over all matters such as murder, rape and deforcement. Below this there is the *Sheriff's Court* which may deal with both indictments and summary complaints. Cases may be referred to the High Court of the Justiciary for sentencing where more severe penalties are required. At the lowest level are the *district courts* which are presided over by magistrates or lay judges and have only a summary jurisdiction.

Criminal prosecutions are brought to the court by the *Procurators-Fiscal* who are under the control of the *Lord Advocate*. They may in certain cases even take charge of the investigation of serious or complex crimes. In jury trials under the *solemn procedure* there are 15 sworn jurors who have to reach a simple majority verdict of guilty, not guilty or not proven. In the *summary procedure* there is no jury and, like the solemn procedure, the accused is permitted to plead guilty, not guilty or that there is no case to answer.

Scottish civil law is divided into two branches: *public law* which deals with administrative and constitutional matters; and *private law* which covers family, delict, contract, property and commercial law. *The Court of Session* in Edinburgh is the senior court which deals with all civil appeals as well as dealing in the first instance with the most important civil cases. Below that the Sheriff's Court deals with all less important cases including those involving sums of money less than £1500.

Actions in the civil courts are started by an initial writ, summons or petition. These will generally be accompanied by a notice of the remedy sought, a statement of the relevant facts called a *condescendence*, and a statement of the legal grounds for the claim to a remedy, called the pleas-in-law. The *defender* may deliver his or her own statement of facts and *pleas-in-law* which may accept or refute that of the *pursuer*. After the service of these pleadings a *closed record* is made by the court which formally defines the allegations, admissions and denials of the parties. The matter is then considered by the court with the evidence being presented before a single judge and any legal arguments subject to debate by counsel.

In the Sheriff's Court there is a small claims procedure for lesser money claims (presently those under £750). In this procedure and in summary causes litigants may act without legal representation by a lawyer. The Sheriff has the freedom to dispense with some of the more formal aspects of the process, making the proceedings quite rapid, easy to use and inexpensive. Self-representation procedures are like those described in Chapters 3 and 4.

Appendix 1

Sample documents

AFFIDAVIT OF SERVICE

I, [*name*] of [*address*] make oath and say as follows:

1. That I am the [plaintiff] [defendant]
2. That I did serve [the summons] [the application] [the document], a true copy of which is attached and marked 'A', on [*person's or company's name*], by delivering it personally to [*name of individual*] at [*full postal address of delivery*] at [*exact time*] on [*date of delivery*].

SWORN AT [*court name*] COUNTY COURT,
this [*date*]
BEFORE ME, [*name of official witness*],
Officer of the Court appointed by the Judge to take Affidavits.

PARTICULARS OF CLAIM (SUBSTANDARD SERVICES)

1. On 7 August 1996 the Plaintiff engaged the services of the Defendants who advertised themselves as a 'professional carpet-cleaning service'.
2. Two days later the Defendants visited the Plaintiff's home and, during the process of cleaning, spoiled an antique Turkish carpet by making the colours run.
3. The Plaintiff refused to pay for the unsatisfactory cleaning service and claims damages from the Defendants for the value of the ruined carpet.
4. The Plaintiff claims the costs of this action.

PARTICULARS OF CLAIM [UNPAID ACCOUNT]

1. The Plaintiff is an experienced decorator.
2. On 11 November 1996 the Defendant contacted the Plaintiff with a request for a quote for some redecoration work.
3. On 13 November 1996 the Plaintiff visited the Defendant's house and gave the Defendant a quote of £1950 for the work including materials.
4. The Defendant accepted the quote and gave the Plaintiff £250 for the purchase of paints, wallpaper and other materials.
5. The redecoration work was commenced on 18 November 1996 and completed 29 November 1996.
6. The Defendant was sent a bill by the Plaintiff for the balance of the account on 1 December 1996 but has failed to settle the account which is now seriously overdue.
7. The Plaintiff claims £1700 damages in respect of the unpaid balance.
8. The Plaintiff also claims interest under section 69 of the County Courts Act 1984 at the rate of 8 per cent per annum from 1 December 1996 to 15 March 1997 being £39.12 and at the daily rate of £0.37 per day up to the date of judgement.
9. The Plaintiff claims the costs of this action.

PARTICULARS OF CLAIM (NEIGHBOUR DISPUTE)

1. The Plaintiff is the leaseholder of the ground floor flat at 12a Wellington Avenue, London NE1.
2. The Defendant resides in the flat above that of the Plaintiff, at 12b Wellington Avenue.
3. Since August 1994 the Plaintiff has suffered intermittent leakages of water from the Defendant's flat, possibly from the Defendant's washing machine which is located above the area where the leaks have occurred.
4. Despite continued complaints to the Defendant the situation has not been remedied.
5. The Plaintiff asks this honourable Court for:
   (i) an injunction to prevent the Defendant from using the said washing machine until it has been replaced or repaired so that it no longer leaks; and
   (ii) damages of £250 for the damage suffered to the Plaintiff's wallpaper, plaster and paintwork below the site of the leak.
6. The Plaintiff claims the costs of this action.

PARTICULARS OF CLAIM (INSURANCE CLAIM)

1. On 27 April 1997 the Plaintiff, took out travel insurance with the Defendant company.
2. The insurance contract was duly completed by the Plaintiff's bank which acted as agent on behalf of the Defendant.
3. On 4 July 1997 while on holiday the Plaintiff suffered the loss by theft of his camera.
4. The loss was reported immediately by the Plaintiff to the insurers as well as to the local police.
5. On 11 July 1997 the Plaintiff formally made a claim on the insurance by returning a completed insurance claim form as required by the contract of insurance.
6. The Defendants have failed to meet the loss and the Plaintiff therefore claims damages of £299, the value of the lost item, plus costs of this action.

Note: Insurance companies, and especially insurance settling agents, are notoriously slow to settle claims. Often court action, or at least the threat of it, is the key to obtaining a prompt and fair settlement.

PARTICULARS OF CLAIM (FAULTY GOODS)

1. On 13 May 1997 the Plaintiff purchased an iron from the Defendant's shop.
2. The iron was expressly sold as having a wide range of temperature settings to suit all fabrics.
3. Later the same day, taking care to follow the instructions that came with it, the Plaintiff used the iron and found that it damaged certain materials.
4. The Plaintiff returned the iron to the shop the next day. The Defendants refused to replace it, refund the money paid or pay compensation for a blouse that had been damaged by the iron.
5. The goods did not match their description nor were they fit for their purpose.
6. The Plaintiff claims damages in respect of the monies paid for the iron [£19.99], the cost of replacing the damaged blouse [£35], and the costs of this action.

Note: The legal criteria for the award of damages in respect of the sale of goods are that the goods must have been not of a 'satisfactory quality' or were 'unfit for the purpose for which they were sold' or that they did not 'match their description'. This covers anything said about the goods, before or at the time of sale, in any sales talk or advertising, or even written on the box or price tag.

PARTICULARS OF CLAIM (GOODS NOT AS DESCRIBED)

1. The Plaintiff is a pensioner who, for many years, has run a small market garden where he grows vegetables both for his own consumption and for sale at market.

2. On 24 April 1997 the Plaintiff purchased some seedlings from the Defendant which were expressly described as being 'hardy and suitable for outdoor planting'.

3. During the following month, despite much care and attention by the Plaintiff, the seedlings failed to take root properly and subsequently died during a period of cold weather.

4. The seedlings did not match their description.

5. The Plaintiff therefore claims from the Defendant:
   (a) £25, the price paid for the seedlings;
   (b) £15, the cost of wasted fertilizers and treatments;
   (c) £50, the estimated loss of profit; and
   (d) costs.

Note: See the note to the previous example.

PARTICULARS OF CLAIM (MOTOR ACCIDENT)

1. The Plaintiff is an experienced driver who has held a full driving licence for 25 years and has 15 years of no claims on his car insurance.
2. On 24 December 1996 the Plaintiff was driving home from work along a familiar route when his car was struck by another car driven by the Defendant.
3. The Defendant who had been driving without due care and attention at excessive speed apparently under the influence of alcohol admitted at the time of the accident to being negligent and at fault and causing the accident.
4. The Plaintiff claims £350 for the cost of repairing the damage caused by the Defendant.
5. The Plaintiff claims the costs of this action.

PARTICULARS OF CLAIM (WRONGFUL DISMISSAL)

1. The Plaintiff is a qualified electrician with 12 years' experience.
2. On 31 December 1996 without warning, the Plaintiff who had held his post employed by the Defendant for 4 years was dismissed. As a result of this the Plaintiff was without income until 1 February 1997 when he started work for another employer.
3. The Plaintiff's dismissal did not follow the procedure described in the contract of employment and no reason was given.
4. The Plaintiff claims £2054 basic pay, overtime and bonuses accrued up to the date of the dismissal which are unpaid plus £2002 basic pay in respect of the period of notice required by the contract plus the costs of this action.

Note: Subject to the terms of any individual contract these particulars of claim could equally be used in the county court where the dismissed person is technically self-employed working on a contract basis, as well as in either the county court or the industrial tribunal where he is an employee. However, if it is wished to remedy the failure to follow proper procedures or to give a reason for the dismissal, or to claim compensation to subsequent career prospects, then the claim becomes one of unfair dismissal at an industrial tribunal. Self-employed persons, however, cannot use the industrial tribunals.

PARTICULARS OF CLAIM (BREACH OF COPYRIGHT)

1. On 1 September 1996 the Plaintiff, a photographer, was invited to participate in a filming session at Richmond Film Recording Studios.

2. No fee was paid to the Plaintiff for this but it was agreed with Mr Middleman, who organised the session, that a fee or royalty would be paid if any photographs she took during the session were ever commercially exploited.

3. In June 1997 photographs taken during the session by the Plaintiff were commercially published by the Defendant in a magazine, large numbers of which were sold to the public.

4. The Plaintiff claims damages to be assessed by the Court for the unauthorized use of her photographs, plus costs.

Note: These particulars of claim could be adapted to cover the unauthorized use, copying, publication or broadcast of most forms of so called 'intellectual property' including written articles, fashion and other designs, computer programs, films, works of art and music, even dramatic and musical performances. To be covered by copyright, intellectual property must be embodied in some permanent form: on paper, on tape, on film or even in the form of data on disk. An idea without any physical embodiment has no copyright.

ORIGINATING APPLICATION
(LANDLORD AND TENANT ACT: MANAGEMENT ORDER)

We, [*name*] of [*address*], [*name*] of [*address*], and [*name*] of [*address*] hereby apply to this honourable Court for the following order:

1. that the Applicants be entitled to manage the Respondent's freehold interest in the premises at [*address of premises*] on such terms as may be agreed between the parties, or, in default of agreement, as determined by this Court or by assessment pursuant to the provisions of the Landlord and Tenant Act 1987;
2. that the Court grant further relief as it sees fit;
3. that the Respondent pay the Costs of this Application.

The persons likely to be affected by this order are as follows:
[*name*] of [*address*] and [*name*] of [*address*]

The grounds on which the Applicants claim to be entitled to this order are:

1. The premises at the stated address subject to the Application, consist of the whole of the building containing 4 flats, 3 of which are held as residential premises by the Applicants.
2. All of the Applicants hold the premises on long leases due to expire in the year 2049.
3. The freehold interest in the premises is held by the Respondent, [*name*] of [*address*].
4. The Respondent landlord is in breach of the repairing covenants in the said leases by failing to undertake necessary repairs, namely, [*details of needed repairs*].
5. The landlord is further in breach of the covenants to insure the property [*give relevant details*].
6. Furthermore, despite these breaches of the covenants, the landlord has continued to levy service charges and contributions in respect of insurance costs.
7. The service charges and rents are insufficient to remunerate a manager.
8. A preliminary notice giving warning of this Application was served on [*date*] by the Applicants on the Respondent requiring him to remedy the said breaches of covenant within 30 days; a copy of this notice is attached hereto.
9. The Respondent has failed to remedy the said breaches of covenant within that time, or at all, and will continue to do so.

Note: These particulars should be signed by all of the Applicants, whose names should also all appear, with the court name and a space for the case number, in the header above the document title. For the purposes of serving the preliminary notice this statement itself could be sent enclosed with a covering letter in this form:

To: [*Respondent's name and address*], Respondent

TAKE NOTICE that we the undersigned, the Applicants in this matter, have the intention to make the enclosed Application in [*County court name*] to be appointed as managing agents of the premises at [*address*].

The Applicants represent a majority of more than two thirds of the qualifying tenants of the premises, all of whom hold leasehold tenancies in excess of 21 years duration and have resided there for 3 years or more.

The grounds on which the order of Court are sought are stated in paragraphs 4 to 6 of the said Application. If, however, within the 30 days following the date of this letter, these grounds cease to exist, then the said Application will not be served on the Court.

Notices in respect of these proceedings shall be served on all persons named in the Application as Applicants or as persons likely to be affected.

Dated   [*date*]

Signed,   _____

          _____
          _____
          _____

          [*all applicants*]

PLAINTIFF'S BILL OF COSTS AS A LITIGANT-IN-PERSON

IN THE _____ COUNTY COURT   CASE NO _____

BETWEEN   _____   (Plaintiff)
and   _____   (Defendant)
and   _____   (Third Party)

Taxed Off			VAT	Expenses	Costs
		The action arose from the sale of an unroadworthy motor vehicle with hidden defects. Damages in respect of the price paid by the Plaintiff were awarded jointly against the Defendant and the Third Party.			rated at £40 ph 2/3rds solicitors' rate of £60 ph
		1. 8/5/96 Issue of Summons: Court fee		£43.00	
		2. 23/5/96 Defence and Third Party Notice			
		3. 7/6/96 Instructions for Discovery, etc			
		4. 21/6/96 Send copy documents: copy fees		£ 2.10	
		5. 7/7/96 Application (copy documents not received)			
		6. 6/9/96 Receive copy documents			
		7. 12/9/96 Send Expert's Report: Expert fee		£80.00	
		8. 26/11/96 Trial Hearing (3hrs plus 59 per cent uplift; travel and waiting time, 2hrs) Witness fee		£50.00	£2.60
		Preparation work: 3 phone calls, 15 letters @approx 0.1hr/item (2hrs); Postage preparation of summons (1hour) preparation of copy documents (20 minutes) preparation of Application (10 minutes) preparation for trial (2 hours 40 minutes) preparation of Bill of Costs (30 minutes) Total preparation work (6 hours 40 minutes)		£5.30	
					£267
		Sub totals		£180.40	£527.00
		Less amount Taxed Off			_____
		Plus Total Expenses			_____
		Plus 7.5% Taxation Fee			_____
		Total			_____

In the _____ County Court   No. of Application _____

IN THE MATTER OF SECTIONS 1 AND 2 OF THE DOMESTIC VIOLENCE AND MATRIMONIAL PROCEEDINGS ACT 1976

BETWEEN   _____ Applicant

and

_____ Respondent

ORIGINATING APPLICATION

I , [*name*] of [*address*], hereby apply for an order that:

The Respondent be restrained from molesting me or the children living with me, or communicating with me or the children other than through a solicitor,

AND that the said order contain a power of arrest,

AND that the Respondent be ordered to pay the costs of this Application.

The grounds on which I claim to be entitled to the order are that the Respondent has attacked me on several occasions, causing me actual bodily harm, and persists in telephoning me and harassing me on my way to and from work. Full particulars of the matter are set out in the Affidavit attached to this Application.

The name and address of the Respondent, on whom it is intended 1that this Application be served, is [*name*] of [*address*]..

My address for the service of documents is [*address*].

Dated [*insert date*]

Signed _____ Applicant

To the District Judge and the Respondent

This application could easily be transformed into an application for an *exclusion order* where the respondent is currently occupying the home, by substituting the following wording for the main clause above:

The Respondent be excluded from the matrimonial home at [*address*] and thereafter be barred from returning there or coming within 100 metres of the boundaries of the property,

AND that I be permitted, with my children, to enter and remain in the said matrimonial home.

The grounds of the application would have to be stated in a similar fashion to those on the non-molestation order application, and be stated more fully in a sworn affidavit. The general form of any affidavit for either type of order is the same as this example of one in support of a non-molestation order:

In the _____ County Court   No. of Application_____

IN THE MATTER OF SECTIONS 1 AND 2 OF THE DOMESTIC VIO-
LENCE AND MATRIMONIAL PROCEEDINGS ACT 1976

BETWEEN _____ Applicant

and

_____ Respondent

AFFIDAVIT

I , [*name*] of [*address*] make oath and say:

1. I, the applicant, was married to the Respondent on the the 6th day of November 1986 at the Registry Office, Wellhampton, Bournshire. There are two children of the marriage aged five and seven. The Respondent is aged 38 and I am aged 36.
2. Since the marriage and until the 14th July 1997 we have lived at the matrimonial home at 6 Wendover Avenue, Wellhampton, Bournshire, which is held as a joint tenancy from Northern Bournland Housing Association. I am employed as a superintendent at a warehouse in Addison Industrial Estate and the Respondent, who is now living at 14 Wychell Gardens, Wellhampton, works as a car mechanic at Slavin's Garage, Wellhampton.
3. During the last year the Respondent has become jealous of me and is obsessed by the idea that I am having an affair with someone else. When he saw me with another man he swore at me and called me a slut and a whore.
4. I have not at any time committed adultery or given the Respondent cause to believe that I have done so.
5. Since February 1997 the Respondent has acted violently towards me and molested me:

   (a) On 6th February 1997 he punched me causing me extensive bruising to my face and body. I did not consult a doctor on this occasion.
   (b) On 27th March 1997 he threatened me with the kitchen knife. In getting away from him I fell and hurt my head which needed six stitches.
   (c) On 12th July 1997 he struck me in the face, kneed me in the stomach and then pushed me up against a wall causing extensive bruising to my back and head. I called the police but they did not want to take any action.

(d) The Respondent left the house on 14th July 1997 but has telephoned me almost daily since then. He always makes abusive remarks and has threatened to hurt me if he sees me with another man.

(e) He painted my car with insulting and abusive comments about me.

(f) He often follows me home from work and pesters me in the street.

6. I am very frightened of the Respondent and I believe he intends to return to our home to harm me or my children.

7. In the circumstances I ask this Honourable Court to grant me its protection by making an order that the Respondent does not molest me.

SWORN this 21st July 1997.

NOTICE OF APPEAL FROM COUNTY COURT

IN THE _____ COUNTY COURT   CASE NO _____

BETWEEN

_____ (Plaintiff)

and

_____ (Defendant)

NOTICE OF APPEAL

TAKE NOTICE that the [Plaintiff] [Defendant] intends to appeal to the Judge at [*address of court*] on [*date*] at [*time*] from the order of District Judge [*name*] given on [*date*].

The grounds of the appeal are as follows

1. [*state ground*]

2. [*state ground*]

3. [*etc*]

Dated _____

Signed _____   [Plaintiff] [Defendant]

NOTICE OF APPEAL FROM MAGISTRATES' COURT

To the Clerk of the Magistrates' Court sitting at [*address*]

and to the Crown Prosecutor, [*address*]

I, [*name*] of [*address*] do hereby give each of you notice that it is my intention to appeal to the Crown Court at [*address*] against [my conviction] [and my sentence] [and the order] made against me by the said Magistrates' Court on the [*date*]

The particulars of the offence with which I was charged related to [*description of charge*] when I was[*describe sentence, verdict, order, etc*]

The general grounds of the appeal are [*state grounds*] [and that I am not guilty of the offence] [and that my sentence was too severe].

Dated _____

Signed _____ Appellant

Appendix 2

Personal injury procedure

Because of the large sums of money involved and the way in which many personal injury cases are fought, I would recommend that professional legal advice always be sought. However, for those of you who have little prospect of obtaining legal representation on terms which are personally acceptable, the following guidelines should help. A pre-proceedings protocol has been agreed between groups of personal injury lawyers and insurance companies and, while it is not strictly binding on litigants-in-person, it is nonetheless advisable to follow it wherever possible.

Cases must be brought by the injured party or a *next friend* where a child or disabled person is involved within three years of the injury. At the time of the accident or as soon as possible thereafter a precise written record needs to be made of what actually happened. This must include details of any immediate ill health, the exact time and location of the accident, how it occurred, who was present at the scene, the registration numbers of any cars involved, weather conditions, etc. Keep any scraps of paper on which contemporaneous notes were taken. Take photos of the location as soon as possible afterwards. If relevant, get details of the workplace and the working practices. Move quickly because often the evidence may be moved, removed or covered up. Prompt court action may allow for the preservation and custody of property by the court (on *ex parte* application). Financial losses must be clearly detailed including the cost of hospital visits, medicines, taxis, etc. Where there has been violent crime it is wise to make a rapid application to the Criminal Injuries Compensation Authority whose address is given in Appendix 3, on p 163.

The first step is to send a letter to the prospective defendant notifying them of your claim. Give details of your identity including your date of birth and National Insurance number, details of the accident, an outline of the injuries suffered and a short concise statement explaining why they are liable. The name and address of your employer, if relevant, and a suggestion that the letter should be passed on to their insurers should also be included. Finally make a request that

1. they provide you with the name of their insurers and the relevant policy number within 28 days and
2. they should indicate whether they accept or deny responsibility within three months.

There is now a standard form of letter which is employed by members of the Association of Personal Injury Lawyers (APIL) and the Association of British Insurers (ABI). Either of these organisations should be able to supply this and details of other protocols which are currently being further developed.

While waiting for a reply to this initial letter you should apply without delay to your doctor or hospital for a medical report, stating that you are prepared to pay an expert's fee (normally £50–£200). You also have the right to instruct an independent specialist expert and if you do it is again advisable to follow the APIL/ABI guidelines. You will need not only to contact the specialist concerned, you will also have to ask your doctor or the hospital concerned to send a copy of your medical records to the expert. I would recommend, however, that wherever possible you restrict the evidence to that of the doctor or specialist who actually treated you at the time of the accident. His report will have much more credibility in the eyes of the judge. By referring to an outside expert you effectively open the door for the opposition to do the same. It is quite common for medical experts instructed by a defendant to come to some quite contrary findings to your own medical expert. Very often these experts will report that they can see 'little in the way of lasting signs and effects of the accident'. Fortunately very few judges now fall for such tactics with the happy result that today most insurers prefer to settle rather than go to court.

If you have been claiming benefit you must contact the Compensation Recovery Unit of the DSS to let them know of your intended action. It is necessary too, in the case of an accident at work, to find out whether the incident was classified as an *industrial accident* by the local Health and Safety Executive office. Your case should be somewhat simplified if the accident was classified in this way. Employers are obliged to report all serious accidents requiring the hospitalisation of an employee or more than three days' sick leave. Sometimes Health and Safety Executive documents will only be released after proceedings are commenced, although you can apply to the court for a pre-proceedings *non-party discovery order* if this causes a problem.

If relevant copies of police reports will be required these can be obtained by visiting the local police station in the area where the accident occurred. Any witnesses should be contacted and statements made. You can get them to swear an affidavit at any court for no charge. Any loss of wages from an employer should be documented for later reference.

Once all of the necessary evidence has been collated and you have heard back from the defendant in respect of the question of liability, the court proceedings can be started. When filling out the summons it is very important to make sure that the legal entity (employer, driver, owner, borough council, etc) who has a responsibility in this matter (eg, for unsafe premises, stairs, pavement, vehicle), or the person who caused the accident by negligence, is clearly identified.

To start an action in the county court you will need to file;

1. a default summons;
2. a statement of claim;
3. a medical report;
4. a schedule of special damages; and
5. the court fee.

The following checklists outline the key facts which must be included in the particulars of claim.

ROAD TRAFFIC ACCIDENT CHECKLIST

1. The identities of the parties involved.
2. The makes, models and registration numbers of any cars, bikes and other vehicles concerned.
3. The location of the accident.
4. The date and time.
5. The directions of travel of the different parties.
6. A description of how the incident happened.
7. Details of related criminal prosecutions, if any.
8. Your date of birth.
9. A medical report describing the injuries sustained.
10. A description of loss of 'amenities'.
11. A summary of the financial damage suffered.

Note that where the driver is uninsured or his identity is uncertain the Motor Insurers' Bureau must be served with a notice of proceedings within seven days of the service of the summons.

WORKPLACE ACCIDENT CHECKLIST

1. The identities of the parties and their work relationship.
2. Your job description.
3. Your place of work.
4. The exact nature of your work.
5. The precise location of the accident.
6. The date and time.
7. A description of how it happened.
8. Your date of birth.
9. A medical report describing the injuries.
10. A description of loss of 'amenities'.
11. A summary of the financial damage suffered.

Any breach of *statutory duty* on the part of the other party should be noted; this includes contravening health and safety regulations under the Factories Act 1961, the Offices, Shops and Railway Premises Act 1963, etc. Details of any negligence should also be included.

After the service of the summons the case will proceed to trial via the standard county court procedure described in Chapter 3. Note that at trial, the principle of *contributory negligence* is important in deciding personal injury cases; for example, the failure to wear a seat belt may count as a 25 per cent contributory negligence in a road traffic accident. The amount of damages awarded will effectively be reduced by such a percentage if the judge finds there have been such contributory factors.

Appendix 3

Useful addresses

The addresses and telephone numbers of your local magistrates' court, Crown Court, county court and family court can be found in your area telephone directory. If you are in any doubt whether any particular court can deal with your enquiry then contact the court nearest to where you live and they will be able to advise you which court to go to. Alternatively you can contact:

Lord Chancellor's Department
Trevelyan House
30 Great Peter Street
London SW1P 2BY
0171-210 3000

The main offices of the High Court and Court of Appeal are at:

Royal Courts of Justice
Strand
London WC2A 2LL
0171-936 6000

Correspondence to the Crown Office should also be sent to the above address and marked for the attention of 'The Master of the Crown Office'.

For all enquiries relating to Industrial Tribunals, including requests for explanatory leaflets and applications forms, contact:

Central Office of the Industrial Tribunals
93 Ebury Bridge Road
London SW1 8RE

For enquiries concerning criminal appeals outside the normal deadlines:

Criminal Cases Review Commission
Alpha Tower
Suffolk Street
Queensway
Birmingham B1 1TT
0121-633 1800

For details of your nearest Citizens Advice Bureau contact:

National Association of Citizens Advice Bureaux
Myddleton House
115–123 Pentonville Road
London N1 9LZ
0171-833 2181

Queries concerning legal aid should be addressed to a solicitor or to:
Legal Aid Board
29/17 Red Lion Street
London WC1R 4PP
0171-405 6991

Legal stationery can be obtained from the company Oyez:
Oyez House
49 Bedford Row
London WC1
0171-242 7132

Details of companies' registered office addresses, trading names, the identity of directors, shareholders and details of accounts and assets can be got from:

Companies House
55–71 City Road
London EC1
0171-253 9393

Companies House
Crown Way
Maindy
Cardiff
01222 380801

Copies of birth and marriage certificates can obtained from your local registry or from:

Registrar-General
St Catherines House
10 Kingsway
London WC2
0171-242 0262

The details of the owner, and of past owners, of any road vehicles can be obtained from:

Driver and Vehicle Licensing Agency
Swansea SA99 1AA
01792 782523

Other organisations which you might need to contact in particular circumstances include:

Association of British Insurers
51 Gresham Street
London EC2V 7HQ
0171-600 3333

Association of Personal Injury Lawyers
33 Pilcher Gate
Nottingham NG1 1QF
0115-958 0585

Advisory, Conciliation and Arbitration Service (ACAS)
Clifton House
83 Euston Road
London NW1 2RB
0171-214 6000

Child Poverty Action Group
1–5 Bath Street
London EC1V 9PY
0171-253 3406

Child Support Agency
DSS Central Office
Newcastle NE98 1YX
0345 133133/0191-225 3154

Commission for Racial Equality
Elliot House
10–12 Allington Street
London SW1 5EH
0171-828 7022

Consumers' Association
14 Buckingham Street
London WC2
0171-839 1222

Criminal Injuries Compensation Authority
Tay House
300 Bath Street
Glasgow G2 4JR
0141-331 2726

Crown Prosecution Service
51 Ludgate Hill
London EC4M 7EX
0171-273 8152

Divorce, Conciliation and Advisory Service
38 Ebury Street
London SW1W 0LU
0171-730 2422

DSS Compensation Recovery Unit
Reyrolle Building
Hebburn
Tyne & Wear NE31 1XB
0191-489 2266

DSS Health and Safety Executive
Broad Lane
Sheffield S3 7HQ
0114-289 2345

Equal Opportunities Commission
Overseas House
Quay Street
Manchester M3 3HN
0161-833 9244

Family and Divorce Centre
162 Tenison Road
Cambridge CB1 2DP
01223 460136

Family Mediators Association
The Old House
Rectory Gardens
Henbury
Bristol BS10 7AQ
0117-962 6300

Law Notes Lending Library
35 Chancery Lane
London WC2A 1NB
0171-405 0780

Law Society
113 Chancery Lane
London WC2A 1LP
0171-242 1222

Legal Action Group
242–4 Pentonville Road
London N1 9UN
0171-833 2931

Legal Services Ombudsman
22 Oxford Ct
Oxford Street
Manchester M23
0161-236 9532

Liberty (National Council for Civil Liberties)
21 Tabard Street
London SE1
0171-403 3888

Mediation UK (an arbitration service)
82a Gloucester Road
Bristol BS7 8BN
0117-924 1234

Motor Insurers' Bureau
152 Silbury Boulevard
Milton Keynes
Beds MK9 1NB
01908 240000

National Council for One-Parent Families
255 Kentish Town Road
London NW5 2LX
0171-267 1361

National Family Mediation
The Chandlery
50 Westminster Bridge Road
London SE1 7QY
0171-721 7658

NSPCC
67 Saffron Hill
London EC1
0171-242 1626
24-hour helpline 0171-404 4447
Childline freephone 0800 1111

Office of Fair Trading
Field House
15/25 Bream's Buildings
London EC4A 1PR
0171-269 8904

Police Complaints Authority
10 Great George Street
London SW7P 3AE
0171-273 6450

Relate
Herbert Gray College
Little Church Street
Rugby
Warks CV21 3AP
01788 573241

Resource Information Service
37 Great Pultney Street
London W1R 3DE
0171-494 2408

Rights of Women
52–54 Featherstone Street
London EC1
0171-251 6577

Shelter
88 Old Street
London EC1V 9AX
0171-253 0202

SHAC
229/231 High Holborn
London WC1V 7DA
0171-404 7447

Women Against Sexual Harassment (WASH)
312 The Chandlery
50 Westminster Bridge Road
London SE1 7QY
0171-721 7593

Appendix 4
Further reading

It is important to bear in mind the fact that the law is continuously developing. This gives rise to frequent changes in statutes, the rules of court and court practice. You should therefore take care to rely on only the most recent, up-to-date, editions of any books you consult. Nearly all specialised law libraries update their collections annually by way of new volumes or supplementary texts. If you have any trouble finding law books, your local public library should be able to advise you of the nearest suitable source.

The following books give full details of current court rules, practice and documents, they are all regularly updated;–

County Court Practice (Butterworths) for county courts, divorce and local family court procedures

Supreme Court Practice (Sweet & Maxwell) for High Court and Court of Appeal procedures

Stone's Justices' Manual for magistrates' court and Crown Court procedures

Another recommended volume which gives a very thorough account of all categories of court action is:

Atkin's Court Forms (Butterworths)

For a simple introduction to much of the law I recommend:

The Penguin Guide to the Law by John Pritchard (Penguin)

For more in-depth reading the best primary source of information is to be found in the volumes of:

Halsbury's Laws of England (Butterworths)

which covers just about every topic possible. This being a 'practitioner's book' is acceptable as a source for quoting the law when presenting legal argument to a court. Butterworths, Sweet & Maxwell, FT Law & Tax, Waterlows and a few other small law publishers publish a whole range of practitioners' books covering all major areas of the law. Where complex matters of law are involved, it may be necessary to refer to the individual law reports of judgements made in actual cases cited in these books. Any library with a specialist law collection will be able to help you find these law reports. Examples of such practitioners' books include:

Murphy (ed.) (1997) *Blackstone's Criminal Practice*, Blackstone, London

Bromley and Lowe (1992) *Bromley's Family Law*, Butterworths, London

(1996) *Cheshire, Fifoot & Furmston's Law of Contract*, Butterworths, London (civil claims)

Bingham *Crown Court Law & Practice*, Kluwer, Netherlands

Rakusen and Hunt (1992) *Distribution of Matrimonial Assets on Divorce*, Butterworths, London

Upex (ed.), *Encyclopaedia of Employment Law*, looseleaf publication, Sweet & Maxwell, London

(1988) *McGregor on Damages* Sweet & Maxwell, London (civil claims)

(1997) *Oke's Magisterial Formulist*, Butterworths, London (magistrates' court)

Other books which may prove helpful are:

Pearce, Nasreen (1991) *Adoption Law and Practice,* Fourmat, London

Moore (1997) *Anthony and Berrymans Magistrates' Court Guide*, Butterworths, London

O'Hare & Hill (1997) *Civil Litigation*, FT Law & Tax, London

Rae, Maggie (1990) *Children and the Law*, Longman, London

Collier, R (1996) *Combatting Sexual Harassment in the Workplace*, Open University, Milton Keynes

Stanesby, Anne (1995) *Consumer Rights Handbook*, Pluto, London

Harries, John (1996) *Consumers: Know your Rights*, Oyez, London

Shackleton and Timbs (1996) *The Divorce Handbook*, Farrar & Co, London

Kibling and Lewis (1996) *Employment Law: Advisor's Handbook*, Legal Action Group, London

Fair Deal, Office of Fair Trading
Priest, J (1993) *Families Outside Marriage*, Family Law, Bristol
Pace, P J (1997) *Family Law*, M&E Handbooks, London
Standley, K (1996) *Family Law*, Macmillan, London
Bird (ed.) (1996) *Family Law Manual*, Sweet & Maxwell, London
Cooklin, S (1989) *From Arrest to Release*, Bedford Square Press, London
Clitheroe *A Guide to Conducting a Criminal Defence*, Oyez, London
National Confederation of Consumer Groups, *A Handbook of Consumer Law*, Which, London
Hill and Redman (1994) *Hill and Redman's Law of Landlord and Tenant*, Butterworths, London
Immigration Law Handbook, Handsworth Law Centre, Birmingham
Marlow *Industrial Tribunals and Appeals*, Bedford Square Press, London
Bower, Jackson and Loughridge (1983) *Living Together*, Century, London
Casson (1996) *Odger's Principles of Pleading*, Sweet & Maxwell, London
Hendy, Day and Buchan (1996) *Personal Injury Practice*, Legal Action Group, London
Buzzard (1997) *Phipson on Evidence*, Sweet & Maxwell, London
Clayton, R (1996) *Practice and Procedure in Industrial Tribunals*, Legal Action Group, London
Stafford (1996) *Private Prosecutions*, Shaw & Sons, London
Grewal, Harjit (1990) *The Sex Discrimination Handbook*, Sphere, London
Keenan (1989) *Smith and Keenan's Mercantile Law*, Pitman, London
Green, D (1995) *Splitting Up*, Kogan Page, London
Cook, MJ (1990) *The Taxation of Legal Costs,* Legal Studies & Services, London
Slade, E (1996) *Tolley's Employment Handbook*, Tolley, London
Tiernan, R (1996) *Tort in a Nutshell*, Sweet & Maxwell, London
(1989) *What to do after an Accident,* Which, London
Rae, Maggie (1990) *Women and the Law*, Longman, London
Malone, Michael (1992) *Your Employment Right*s, Kogan Page, London
Richards, K (1996) *350 Legal Problems Solved*, Which, London

Glossary

Action Any type of civil proceedings including family matters; see Chapter 1, pp 1–2 for the distinction between civil and criminal law.

Admissible Evidence which to the judge appears to be allowable under the rules of court.

Affidavit A written statement of fact made by a witness. Affidavits must be signed after swearing an oath as to the truth of the contents. See Chapter 3, pp 36–7.

Alibi A defence to a criminal charge based on the accused being elsewhere when the crime was committed.

Application A formal request to the court for any order, applications may be *originating* or *interlocutory*.

Arbitration A less formal alternative to trial proceedings which is used for *small claims* in the county court; see Chapter 3, pp 56–60.

Attachment of earnings An order of court to an employer to deduct and pay to the court monies owed by an employee in respect of a court judgement against them.

Bail The release from custody between arrest and trial of a charged person, often subject to strict conditions including the deposit of a sum of money forfeited if that person absconds.

Bailiff An officer of a court with responsibility for enforcing court orders.

Bill of costs A summary detailing the work carried out on a legal matter, a bill of costs can be challenged in court where it appears to be excessive.

Breach of contract   A failure to honour the terms of any agreement.

Burden of proof   The requirement to convince the court of what you say is truth.

Case law   See *Common law*.

Cause lists   Daily listings put up in each courthouse giving details of the courtroom and approximate time allocations for the cases being heard that day.

Chambers   In private hearing, with the public excluded.

Circuit judge   A full-time judge who sits in the county court and Crown Court.

Common law   Law which has a traditional rather than a statutory basis; see Chapter 1, pp 4–7.

Complaint   The first stage of civil procedure in the magistrates' court; see Chapter 4, pp 83–8.

Constructive dismissal   The situation where an employee is forced to resign because of unbearable conditions.

Contempt of court   A criminal charge brought for any serious failure to respect the orders and rules of court.

Contentious   Legal matters which involve direct court action against another party or which are otherwise disputed.

Contributory negligence   The situation in civil law where the wronged party is in part to blame for the wrong.

Costs   The cost of the legal work carried out in relation to any matter of law.

Costs in cause   An order that the costs of any *interlocutory* matter will be assessed at the end of proceedings in favour of the successful party.

Counterclaim   A claim made by a *defendant* against a *plaintiff* in response to the latter's claim against the former.

Cross-examination   The questioning of a witness by the opposing side.

Cross-appeal   A second appeal made in response to a first appeal made by another party.

Damages   Monetary compensation.

Decree absolute   The definitive grant of a divorce.

Decree nisi   A grant of divorce waiting to be finalised.

Default judgement   A judgement that is entered by the court where no defence or notice of intention to defend a case has been delivered by the *defendant*.

Defence   A *defendant*'s response to the case against him.

Defendant   The party defending an action.

Discovery   The court procedures for the disclosure of documents and other evidence.

District judge   A junior judge who deals with *small claims* and other day-to-day procedural matters in the county court.

Entrapment   The active trapping of a suspect by the police.

Equity   The application of the principles of justness and fairness to court judgements.

Ex parte   Without notice to other involved parties.

Examination-in-chief   The questioning of a witness by the party which called that witness.

Execution   The carrying out of a court order.

Expert witness   A witness who delivers an opinion rather than strictly factual evidence.

Filing of documents   The delivery of documents to the court.

Frustration   The situation where a contract becomes impossible to carry out because of external circumstances.

Garnishee order   An order intercepting money owed to a defendant to satisfy a judgement against him.

Hearsay   Indirect "second-hand" testimony which is allowed to be put before a court in certain circumstances; see Chapter 3, pp 65–6.

Inadmissible   Evidence which is not allowed to be given by virtue of the rules of court.

Indictment   A written accusation of charges which is read out at the start of a Crown Court trial; see Chapter 4, pp 83–90.

Industrial accident   An accident at work officially recognised by the Health and Safety Executive.

Injunction   A court order forbidding a named person to do something.

Interlocutory   A interim matter arising during proceedings.

Interpleader   A court procedure to establish who has the best claim to any property held by an independent party or by the court bailiffs.

Judicial separation   A rarely used means of a married couple formally separating without a divorce; see Chapter 5, p 104.

Jurisdiction   The areas within which a court is empowered to act.

Law report   A published report of a court case.

Laying information   The preliminary stage of criminal proceedings in the magistrates' court; see Chapter 4, pp 84–8.

Leading question   A question that infers or limits its answer.

Leave of court   Permission obtained from a court allowing something to be done.

Limitation   The imposition of time limits on bringing any case to court; normally six years for most civil matters, three years for personal injury cases and six months for summary offences. More serious criminal offences are subject to no such time limits.

Liquidated damages   Damages, the amount of which can be exactly calculated; *unliquidated damages* by contrast cannot be calculated in terms of any specific amount and thus is left to the court to decide.

Litigant   A party or person involved in a court action.

Mitigating circumstances   Factors that appear to lessen the culpability of criminal offender.

Mitigation   A *plaintiff*'s obligation to limit damages; see Chapter 3, pp 67–8.

Negligence   Failure to observe a duty of care towards others; a type of *tort*.

Non-contentious   Legal matters which are not *contentious*.

Obiter dictum   Things said as an aside by a judge when delivering judgement; see *ratio decidendi*.

Open court   Court proceedings on which the public may spectate.

Originating application   An *application* which is made to the court independent of any existing court case.

Ouster   An order excluding a spouse from a home.

Particulars   Written details of any *pleading*.

Payment into court   Money paid into court to settle any monetary claim made against a *defendant*; the whole sum claimed or a lesser sum may be offered.

Pending suit   An interim order made by the court that has effect until a final judgement is delivered.

Perjury   Making a false statement on oath or in an official document.

Personal injury   An injury to a person in or out of work.

Petitioner   The person who delivers a (divorce) petition to the court; see Chapter 5, pp 101–8.

Plaintiff   The party bringing a claim against another in civil proceedings.

Pleading   The written details of any claim or defence.

Pre-trial review   An *interlocutory* hearing at which a *district judge* will usually give procedural directions; see Chapter 3, pp 32–3.

Precedent   The authority of a previous judgement of one of the senior courts which judges in the lower courts are bound to follow; see Chapter 1, pp 4–7.

Prosecutor   The person who brings a criminal charge against another in court.

Ratio decidendi   The reasoning behind any judgement delivered by a judge.

Recorder   A part-time judge who usually sits in the county court, Crown Court or family court.

Re-examination   The final stage of *examination-in-chief* when the party calling a witness can address any issues raised during *cross-examination*; see Chapter 3, pp 62–4.

Reserved judgement   A decision not delivered at the trial hearing but instead is to be delivered later, often in writing.

Respondent   The person replying to an *application* or *petition*.

Section   A numbered paragraph in a *statute*.

Secured   Guaranteed by way of a provision against property.

Service of documents The delivery of documents to the court and to any other party to any court proceedings as required by the rules of court or an order of court.

Set aside To render void.

Small claim A claim for under £3000 in the county court dealt with by an *arbitration*-like procedure; see Chapter 3, pp 56–60.

Special damage A specific rather than a general financial loss.

Specific performance An order of court that a person must carry out a particular act; any failure to do so is punishable as *contempt of court.*

Statute An Act of Parliament which is a written embodiment of the Law; see Chapter 1, pp 4–7.

Statutory duty An obligation under the law to do something, eg the provision of safe work premises.

Stay of execution A period during which an order of the court cannot be enforced, so as to allow an appeal by the party against whom the order is made.

Struck out Disallowed.

Sub judice Under judicial consideration, or in other words, when a matter is the subject of court proceedings. There are strict regulations on the reporting of cases that are before the courts to prevent any biasing of a jury and to protect the privacy of parties involved in various categories of family proceedings.

Subpoena A summons compelling a witness to attend court to give evidence or to produce specific documents.

Summary judgement A judgement made without there being a full Trial, generally awarded only where it appears that a party has no real hope of winning a case. See also *Default judgement.*

Summons A call to court which is the first stage of many types of court proceedings. In the magistrates' court a date and time to attend the court will be specified, whereas in the county court a written reply is requested.

Taxation of costs The procedure where the *costs* of the successful party in a case are assessed by the court.

Third party A party other than a *plaintiff* or *defendant* involved in court proceedings.

Third party notice   A form of *pleading* employed wherein a *defendant* asserts that a *third party* has ultimate responsibility for a claim made against him. Upon receipt the third party becomes a party to the proceedings and may file a defence to the third party notice.

Tort   A civil (rather than a criminal) wrong, other than a breach of contract. Torts include defamation, nuisance and negligence and are actionable for damages, injunctions, etc, in the civil courts.

Unfair contract   A contract with terms so unreasonable that a court will not enforce every clause.

Unfair dismissal   A dismissal from employment which is either unreasonable or procedurally wrong.

Unliquidated damages   Damages to which a direct monetary value cannot easily be assigned; see *Liquidated damages*.

Warrant of execution   An order of court for goods belonging to a debtor to be seized by bailiffs.

Witness summons   The common name for a *subpoena*.

Writ   The first stage of civil proceedings in the High Court. A *defendant* must acknowledge receipt of a *writ*; otherwise *summary judgement* may be entered.

Wrongful dismissal   A dismissal which is brought without respect to proper notice periods or other terms of the contract of employment; see Chapter 6, p 119.

Index

repossession proceedings 14, 25
respondent 32, 101, 105
right of silence 81, 82

searches by police 77–83
sentence 84, 87, 88, 93, 130, 132, 133, 134
service of documents 29, 45, 49, 83, 104–6, 129, 130, 132, 133, 138
setting aside 29, 95, 111
setting down for trial 41
settling out of court 40–1, 61
sexual discrimination and harassment 120–1
skeleton arguments 130–1
small claims 8, 22–3, 56–8, 115, 125, 128
social security appeals 126–7
solicitors 3, 8, 9, 12–17, 45, 51, 55–6, 57, 60, 67, 80, 81, 82, 99, 100, 108, 109, 114, 125
special damage 28
specific performance 32
statement of claim 74
  see also particulars
stating a case 129, 130, 132, 133
statutes 4–7, 53, 55, 66
statutory charge 13, 100, 102
statutory duty 32, 159
stay of execution 69
striking out 38, 39–40, 41
sub-judice 28
submissions of legal argument 37, 56, 96
substandard services 139
summary judgement 29, 39–40, 46
summary proceedings 76, 84
summing up 79, 87, 92
summons 23, 24–9, 35, 45, 56, 76, 83, 95–6, 97, 158
Supreme Court 24, 73, 131, 132, 133

see also Court of Appeal: High Court

tax on maintenance payments 111
taxation of costs 69–70
third party proceedings 21, 31–2, 62, 66, 68
time limits 20–1, 101, 115, 116, 122, 129, 130, 156
trade unions 17, 115
triable in either way 76, 84
trial 43, 51–4, 56–67, 83, 129–32
tribunals 115–27
tort 20

unfair dismissal 116, 118–19
unliquidated damages 28
unpaid debts 20, 140
unsatisfactory goods and services 20, 143, 144

verdict 79, 87, 90, 92, 93, 134
violence 101, 109, 113–14, 118, 151–3

wages, unpaid 28, 119
warrant for arrest 83
warrant of execution (bailiffs) 23, 71
without prejudice 40
witness 42–3, 52–4, 57, 59, 62–5, 82, 86, 89, 92, 94, 96, 106, 125, 126
  character 87, 92
  expert 42–3
  identification 79, 81, 96
witness costs 23, 42
witness statement or summary 42–5, 48, 54–65, 88
witness summons/order 42–3, 48, 54, 87, 89, 94
writ 73, 80
wrongful dismissal 119, 146